ARISTOTLE'S POLITICAL
THEORY

ARISTOTLE'S POLITICAL THEORY

An Introduction for Students of Political Theory

BY

R. G. MULGAN

CLARENDON PRESS · OXFORD

Oxford University Press, Walton Street, Oxford OX2 6DP
Oxford New York Toronto
Delhi Bombay Calcutta Madras Karachi
Petaling Jaya Singapore Hong Kong Tokyo
Nairobi Dar es Salaam Cape Town
Melbourne Auckland
and associated companies in Beirut Berlin Ibadan Nicosia

Oxford is a trade mark of Oxford University Press

Published in the United States
by Oxford University Press, New York

First published 1977
Reprinted 1986, 1987

British Library Cataloguing in Publication Data
Mulgan, R. G.
Aristotle's political theory.
1. Aristotle—Politics
I. Title
320   JC71.A7   77–30161
ISBN 0–19–827416–5 Pbk

Printed in Great Britain by
Biddles Ltd, Guildford & King's Lynn

CONTENTS

REFERENCES AND QUOTATIONS

References to the *Politics* are given in the form III.12.i (1282 ^{b} 14–18) 127–8. These figures relate to the number of book, chapter, and section (III.12.i), the page, column, and line number in the classic Berlin edition of Aristotle's works (1282 ^{b} 14–18), both of which are reproduced in Ernest Barker's translation published by Oxford University Press, and the page number in the Penguin translation by T. A. Sinclair (127–8). References to other works of Aristotle give the name of the work (the standard abbreviation *EN* is used for the *Nicomachean Ethics*), the book and chapter, and the page, column, and line in the Berlin edition.

Footnotes have been restricted to references to Aristotle's works. Modern works about Aristotle are referred to in notes collected at the end of the book.

Quotations from the *Politics* are from Sinclair's translation, occasionally amended; quotations from other works of Aristotle are from the Oxford translations, edited by J. A. Smith and W. D. Ross.

INTRODUCTION

Courses in the history of political thought often, and rightly, begin with the two most important works of Greek political theory, Plato's *Republic* and Aristotle's *Politics.* Of the two the *Politics* is much the more difficult to appreciate. Unlike the *Republic*, which is an undoubted literary masterpiece, it is a disjointed collection of different essays, some of them incomplete and none of them intended to be read outside the circle of Aristotle and his students. The modern reader looking for expert guidance will be disappointed because modern scholarship has tended to neglect the *Politics* except as a source for Greek history or for Aristotle's philosophical development. This book is a modest attempt to help redress the balance. It is intended for students of political theory who are meeting the *Politics* for the first time and in an English translation. It does not offer a complete introduction to the work but assumes some elementary knowledge of Aristotle's life and times, his intellectual background and the social and political structure of the Greek city state. The main aim is to bring the major themes and arguments of Aristotle's political theory into sharper focus than they appear in the *Politics* itself. To achieve this within a reasonable compass, one must abandon the expectation that an account of Aristotle's political theory will be an analysis of all the arguments of the *Politics* in the order in which they appear in the text. This study makes no claim to be complete. Moreover, though the list of topics discussed, chapter by chapter, roughly follows the major divisions of the *Politics*, arguments on the same topic from different parts of the *Politics*, as well as from other works of Aristotle, are discussed together. Such a procedure assumes that the *Politics* reflects a unified and coherent body of political theory, an assumption rejected by those Aristotelian scholars who attribute different books or sections to different stages in the development of Aristotle's philosophy and approach to political theory. But the major differences between sections of the *Politics* can be explained more economically by the fact that different topics give rise to different questions; there is no compelling need to assume differences in date or philosophical doctrine. Inconsistencies will still be found and we shall still sometimes want to say that Aristotle's thought has developed or that he has changed his mind. On the whole, however, cross-reference from one section of the *Politics* to another leads to corroboration much more often than to contradiction and so vindicates the general assumption of unity.

It is also assumed that the history of political thought is not a merely antiquarian study but involves critical reflection on a living tradition. The ideas of an ancient writer like Aristotle are to be understood within their historical context but must also be tested against our own experience and values. Explicit criticism concentrates, though not exclusively, on internal inconsistencies within Aristotle's doctrines, but the ideas and arguments, it is hoped, have been presented in such a way that the reader will readily find himself drawing modern parallels or offering his own assent or dissent. Such a response, he may be sure, is what Aristotle would have expected and is what his writings deserve.

CHAPTER ONE

HUMAN GOOD AND POLITICAL SCIENCE

'Politics', for Aristotle, implies the *polis,* the Greek city state. Though he knew of forms of community other than the *polis* and though the continuing relevance of his political theory depends on our ability to apply it to quite different types of state, he is concerned almost exclusively with the sort of community in which he spent his life. The Greek *polis* provided a unique type of civilized life and Aristotle considers it indispensable for the full development of human potential. Indeed, it is the development of this potential, the achievement of human good, which is the aim of political science, the science of the *polis.* The ethical purpose of political science is described in the opening chapters of the *Nicomachean Ethics.* (Of Aristotle's two ethical treatises, the *Eudemian* and the *Nicomachean Ethics,* the latter is more closely connected with the *Politics* and of greater relevance for his political theory. For convenience we shall refer to it simply as the '*Ethics*'.) Political science is the 'architectonic' or master discipline, which exercises general control over all other disciplines.

For it is this that ordains which of the sciences should be studied in a state, and which each class of citizens should learn and up to what point they should learn them; and we see even the most highly esteemed of capacities fall under this, e.g. strategy, economics, rhetoric.[1]

Because its authority is supreme and because it directs the activities of other disciplines, each of which is concerned with one particular area of human activity, its aims or purpose must be similarly all-embracing.

Now since political science uses the rest of the sciences, and since, again, it legislates as to what we are to do and what we are to abstain from, the end of this science must include those of the other sciences, so that its end must be the good for man.[2]

Political science thus aims at the whole of human good, not just for isolated individuals but for all the members of a community.[3] An account of Aristotle's political theory must therefore begin with his conception of human good.

[1] *EN* I.2 (1094 a 28–b 3).
[2] *EN* I.2 (1094 b 4–7); cf III.12. i (1282 b 14–18) 127–8.
[3] *EN* I.2 (1094 b 7–10).

Human Good

Following standard Greek usage Aristotle identifies human good with *eudaimonia* which means 'happiness' or, better, 'the good life'. *Eudaimonia,* as he describes it in the *Ethics,* involves the exercise of two types of virtue, ethical and intellectual. In his account of the ethical virtues,[4] Aristotle remains close to the values of Greek society and especially to those of its well-educated and well-to-do male members. The man of ethical virtue is brave in battle (courage), honest in his business dealings (justice), and generous to his city and his friends (magnificence, liberality); he has a proper estimate of his own value in the community (magnanimity, proper ambition) though he need not necessarily participate in the government of the community; he is of even temper (good temper) and is a reliable and congenial companion (friendliness, truthfulness, and ready wit); though he keeps his physical desires under proper control, he does not suppress them altogether (temperance).

In addition to an ethically virtuous disposition, the happy man must have a certain amount of what Aristotle calls 'external goods'.[5] Such things as health, wealth, and friends are not good in themselves but they are often necessary as means or instruments for the exercise of virtue. For example, generosity requires wealth with which to be generous; friendliness cannot be displayed unless one has friends. Furthermore, a certain level of good fortune is essential.

There are some things the lack of which takes the lustre from happiness, such as good birth, goodly children, beauty.[6]

But happiness does not require more than a modest level of such external goods. 'We can do without ruling earth or sea.'[7] This is a good example of how Aristotle starts from generally accepted views and then criticizes and refines them without rejecting them altogether. Some philosophers claimed that virtue alone was necessary for happiness and that external goods were quite irrelevant. Many Greeks, on the other hand, identified the good life with the possession of such things as money, noble birth, and power. Aristotle takes a middle course. To claim that material well-being and good fortune have no bearing on whether or not one is happy is too paradoxical and contrary to experience. Yet to equate happiness with the possession of wealth and honour conflicts with Aristotle's philosophical belief that the aim of human life

---

[4] *EN* II–V.   [5] *EN* I.8 (1099 a 31–b 8); X.8 (1178 b 33–5).
[6] *EN* I.8 (1099 b 2–3).   [7] *EN* X.8 (1179 a 4).

is to develop the potentiality for virtue implied by man's unique characteristic, reason. Thus he arrives at a compromise which will satisfy both theory and facts: happiness implies virtue but a minimum of external goods is an essential auxiliary.

As well as ethical virtue and external goods the good life also includes the intellectual virtues. Apart from 'practical wisdom' (*phronesis*) which is involved in ethically virtuous behaviour, the intellectual virtue most relevant to human happiness is 'wisdom' (*sophia*) which has nothing to do with the variable sphere of human action but concentrates on eternal and unchanging objects.[8] In determining the role of wisdom in the good life, Aristotle again strikes a balance between the views of philosophers and those of ordinary Greeks. As a young man he had been influenced by Plato's arguments in favour of the philosophical life and in all his ethical writings we find him arguing that philosophical contemplation is the highest and best human activity. In the *Ethics* he postpones discussion of the theoretical or contemplative life till the end of the last book,[9] where he gives several reasons for the supremacy of contemplation: reason is the best part of man; contemplation is the most continuous and the most pleasant activity; the philosopher has least need of external goods; contemplation is the only thing loved for its own sake and is the only truly divine activity. Such arguments may seem to imply that there is no value in any activity other than philosophical contemplation and that the ethical virtues are to be completely ignored. But this is not Aristotle's intention. He claims that a life of pure contemplation would be 'too high for man'.[10] Man is only partly, not wholly, divine. The exercise of the highest part of his reason can therefore occupy only part of his life. In so far as the philosopher is a man and lives with other people, he must choose to do acts of ethical virtue.[11] Ethical virtues which correspond to our less divine and more human capacities, will be essential for human happiness, though to a secondary degree.[12]

Aristotle's conclusion is thus another compromise. Human happiness entails a mixture of contemplation and ethical virtue. Contradictions still remain between the two sets of values and some of the arguments in favour of the contemplative life still prove too much. But we should not be misled by such inconsistencies or by the position of the discussion at the end of the *Ethics* into thinking that it has been tacked on as a pious but incongruous epilogue. There is no evidence that Aristotle ever

[8] *EN* VI.7. [9] *EN* X.7–8. [10] *EN* X.7 (1177 b 26–7).
[11] *EN* X.8 (1178 b 5–6). [12] *EN* X.8 (1178 a 9).

abandoned the ideal of the philosophical life. Though he could not bring himself to support it unconditionally, he was equally unwilling to reject it altogether and we should accept this mixed ideal as his final account of the nature of the good life. The happy man will be someone who values the philosophical contemplation of eternal truths above all else and will devote a considerable amount of his time to it. But he will also live a full social life in the company of his family and friends and will enjoy a moderate amount of wealth and good fortune.

Aristotle's ideal is necessarily exclusive; it cannot be achieved by all inhabitants of a *polis*. Philosophical ability, he assumes, is relatively rare and can certainly not be found in everyone. More important, the exercise of the virtues, both intellectual and ethical, requires a degree of leisure and material prosperity which, given the economic and technical conditions of Greek society, depends upon the exertions of others who are thereby excluded from the life of virtue. In fairness to Aristotle we must remember that he is reflecting the attitudes of his own society. The assumption that only a few can live a happy and good life would have seemed self-evident to most of his contemporaries who would have been startled and shocked by the suggestion that happiness should be enjoyed by all.

This conception of the good life provides the background and inspiration for most of Aristotle's political theory. The connection between his ethical ideals and his political science is most clearly expressed in the last chapter of the *Ethics,* where, having completed his account of the good life, he raises the question of how it is to be implemented. People are unlikely to become good unless the government and the laws are directed towards the achievement of human good. The complete 'philosophy of human nature' must therefore include the study of laws and constitutions and how best to frame them.[13] The chapter finishes with a list of topics which foreshadows, though not with complete accuracy, the contents of the *Politics.*[14] The influence of Aristotle's ethics on his politics will be most apparent in his discussion of the nature of the *polis* and in his account of the ideal state which is intended to implement the ethical ideal. But it also extends into that part of his political theory which deals with the politics of the ordinary Greek *polis.* Though it may not be possible to create an ideal state governed by truly good men dedicated to providing the good life for all who are capable of achieving it, in the ordinary Greek city state a group

[13] *EN* X.9 (1181 b 12–15).
[14] *EN* X.9 (1181 b 15–24).

of well-educated and like-minded friends might still be able to live Aristotle's good life. They would not need to take part in the government of their community; the good life does not require such participation. They would simply need a government which would preserve their lives, property, and general good fortune while they lived the life of the intellectual and ethical virtues. Their main political demands would thus be security and stability which, as we shall see, are the major values and objectives assumed by Aristotle in his treatment of everyday, non-ideal politics.

Political Science

That the study of politics, especially when it involves the explicit pursuit of ethical objectives, can be called a 'science' may surprise the modern reader who is used to a much narrower conception of science. Aristotle's view of scientific explanation is less restricted than ours and embraces not only the 'efficient' or moving cause, which comes closest to the modern notion of scientific cause, but also the 'material' cause, which refers to the material or matter of which the object consists, the 'final' cause, which is the goal or end towards which the object is moving, and the 'formal' cause, which is the essential nature or 'form' of the object. He would count as a science (*episteme*) any body of statements which gives such explanations about a particular subject matter provided that the explanations are general in form and derive from certain principles or 'starting-points'. These criteria are very flexible and imprecise and make it difficult to tell whether or not a given intellectual study is a science. Such a difficulty does not worry Aristotle, who is interested more in identifying the points of difference between intellectual disciplines than in drawing a sharp line between scientific and non-scientific knowledge. In the case of political science, this approach is particularly valuable. It avoids the arid and ultimately unrewarding problem of whether political science really is a science and directs us to the much more fruitful question of how far and in what respects political science differs from other sciences.

From disciplines such as mathematics and astronomy political science diverges in two important respects. The first is the degree of accuracy to be expected in its conclusions. Aristotle believes that in any subject we should expect only that degree of certainty which the subject matter allows.

It is the mark of the educated man to look for precision in each class of things just so far as the nature of the subject admits; it is evidently equally foolish to accept probable reasoning from a mathematician and to demand from a rhetorician logical proofs.[15]

The subject matter of political science is human action. This precludes the certainty of mathematics because one cannot make general statements about human behaviour to which there will be no exceptions. Such generalizations are true 'for the most part' or 'in general' but not true 'absolutely' or 'without qualification'. One reason for this uncertainty in human affairs is that human actions are products of deliberate choice and so are in some sense outside the necessary chains of cause and effect. As actions are chosen they are unpredictable and so certainty about what will happen is impossible. For Aristotle, however, sciences dealing with human behaviour are not the only sciences in which it is impossible to make certain predictions. Some of the physical and the biological sciences are also subject to uncertainty because none of the objects in our world, animate or inanimate, has the certainty and necessity which belong to the objects of mathematics or to the movements of the heavenly bodies. Aristotle is therefore not a determinist in the natural sciences and his acceptance of deliberate or 'free' behaviour in human beings does not create a gulf between the study of human behaviour and that of other natural phenomena. Without a belief in scientific determinism, 'free will' is a much less significant or contentious phenomenon.

Secondly, political science differs in its aims, and it is this difference rather than their comparative lack of precision, which distinguishes sciences of human behaviour from other sciences. Subjects such as metaphysics, mathematics, and physics (which for Aristotle embraces the whole field of what we would call natural science, both physical and biological) are 'theoretical' sciences because they are pursued purely for reasons of disinterested scientific inquiry. Political science, however, like ethics, economics, and rhetoric, is a 'practical' science because its aim is to determine how one ought to act. 'The end is not knowledge but action.'[16] Aristotle's main purpose in the *Politics* is not to give an academically dispassionate account of political phenomena but to provide a handbook or guide for the intending statesman; 'political science' (*politike*) is also 'statesmanship'. Though Aristotle sometimes admits to a more disinterested and academic view of the subject's aims,[17] in general the questions he raises and the

---

[15] *EN* I.3 (1094 b 23–7); cf. VII.7.ix (1328 a 19–21) 270.
[16] *EN* I.3 (1095 a 5–6); cf. *EN* II.2 (1103 b 26–9); *EN* X.9 (1179 a 35–b 7).
[17] III.8.i (1279 b 12–15) 116.

answers he gives to them are directly related to the aim of instructing those in power. True, the general tone of much of the *Politics* is dispassionate and, though this may be partly due to the fact that the *Politics* is made up of lecture or research notes and was not intended for publication, we may suspect that Aristotle's own interest in studying politics is as much academic as practical. But this detachment of tone is not necessarily inconsistent with the view that political science is practical in purpose. The description 'practical' refers to the structure of the science, which will lead to conclusions about how to act, rather than to the motives or intentions of the political scientists themselves. Like all the major Greek political theorists, Aristotle is writing primarily for the ruler, the statesman or legislator who will be making important political decisions, rather than for the ordinary citizen; his political science is statesmanship not civics. In this respect Greek political theory differs from the main modern tradition of political theory which has been more concerned with the interests of the individual subject and his relation to the state.

The overtly practical purpose of Aristotle's political science explains the close dependence of the *Politics* on his conception of human good. Political decisions must be based not only on knowledge about the workings of politics but also on some view of the ends or goals which the community ought to be pursuing. Some modern political scientists would claim that discussion of human values and ideals must be avoided. One may quite legitimately observe and try to explain the facts of political life, such as the nature of political institutions and how people behave within them, but questions about how such institutions and behaviour ought to be conducted belong to the realm of values and cannot be scientifically determined. Value judgements, it is held, are matters of choice or preference and not of knowledge. Aristotle, however, does not accept any such sharp logical distinction between facts and values. He believes that one can have knowledge, and be right and wrong, about what we call questions of value. None the less, he does admit that the answers to such questions are not of precisely the same logical status as propositions in the theoretical sciences. Political science involves a different type of intellectual process which Aristotle calls *phronesis*, usually translated as 'practical wisdom'. The nature of *phronesis* is not completely clear but it seems to involve the knowledge of the correct ends or values as well as the calculation of the correct means to these ends. It includes the ability to assess the particular characteristics of unique, individual situations and also to grasp general principles of conduct. Though it is an intellectual faculty it is not purely intellectual and depends, at least in part, on having the right moral education and experience. The man of practical wisdom is like our man of 'good judgement', the man who combines intellectual ability with the character and experience necessary to make wise and sensible decisions in particular human situations. By making the right character and experience components of practical wisdom, Aristotle recognizes an important difference between questions involving evaluation and choice and questions in the theoretical sciences. Recognition of this difference ought perhaps to have led him to qualify his assumption that answers to questions of value can be objectively right or wrong. Yet the view that political science should include discussion of human values should not be rejected out of hand. Certain objectively determinable evidence about human behaviour is relevant to political aims and values. Though we may disagree with the evidence that Aristotle finds or with the way he uses it, we should not object to his general assumption that political ideals and judgements of political value are to be based on facts of human behaviour.

The dependence of political science on the right character and experience means that it is not a subject to be taught to the inexperienced young.[18] Such an attitude may shock the modern student but he should remember that, because Aristotle's political science is a practical science, proficiency in it means more than just being able to write or talk well about politics in general terms, as Aristotle himself does in the *Politics*; it also implies being able to act correctly in particular political situations. The ultimate test of competence in political science will be practical not academic and we are more likely to recognize the need for character and experience in practical than in theoretical matters. Furthermore, child prodigies, though not uncommon in the sciences and mathematics, are virtually unknown in the humanities, which tends to support the view that even the purely academic understanding of political behaviour requires personal experience of human action.

Political science is thus a science with a difference. It is practical rather than theoretical in purpose and requires character and experience as well as intellectual ability. Its fundamental principles or 'starting-points' will be the goals which the statesman ought to achieve; next will come certain generalizations or rules about how these goals are to be

---

[18] *EN* 1.3 (1095 a 2–6); *EN* X.9 (1181 a 9–12).

achieved in different types of political situation; finally, the rules will
be applied to actual situations. This is the type of structure that we
should expect from Aristotle's account of the nature of political
science and of science in general and, in broadest outline, it is the
structure he adopts in his written works. Goals are discussed in the
ethical treatises and means to these goals in the *Politics*, while the
final stage of action is necessarily not described but left to be acted.
Within each work, however, Aristotle does not always follow the
prescribed pattern of progression from the more general and fundamental of the more specific and particular. The method or pattern
which a science will follow in its final, completed form must be distinguished from the method of scientific inquiry used in discovering
this pattern. Most of Aristotle's surviving writings, including those on
ethics and politics, are concerned with this preliminary task of scientific
investigation rather than with final exposition.

Aristotle's methods of inquiry are flexible and varied but certain
elements constantly recur: first, a statement of problems or difficulties
arising in connection with a particular topic and a summary of the
relevant views of others, either philosophers or laymen; then an attempt
to resolve the difficulties by adducing new evidence or introducing new
distinctions while trying as far as possible to preserve the views of others.
This type of argument, sometimes known as the 'aporetic' method
(from the Greek *aporia*, meaning 'problem' or 'difficulty') is common
in the *Politics*, especially in Books One, Three, and Four. The arguments
are often difficult to follow because the direction of the argument
seems to change frequently and because we are sometimes not sure
whether Aristotle is merely reporting the views of someone else or
actually subscribing to them himself. His use of this method illustrates
an important aspect of his approach to all sciences, including political
science. He has a great respect for what he observes, for 'phenomena',
which includes not only what he has seen in the world around him but
also what he has heard from others. Any valid scientific theory or
generalization must incorporate or harmonize with most if not all such
phenomena. This respect for what he has seen and heard helped him to
reject Plato's theory of transcendent forms or ideas with its accompany-
ing contempt for the world of the senses. It also makes him deeply
conservative and anti-radical, in a general and not just a political sense,
because he is unwilling to stray too far from what is accepted or acceptable.[19] Such an attitude of mind, as we shall see, is of ambiguous value

---

[19] Cf. II.5.xvi (1264 ^{a} 1–5) 65.

in his political theory. It keeps him from supporting certain impractical and potentially dangerous proposals, yet there are occasions when we wish that he would let the logic of his argument run further and reveal the inconsistency or injustice in a cherished institution or practice.

CHAPTER TWO

THE POLIS

Like any other Aristotelian science, political science in its finished form will begin with certain basic principles. Aristotle therefore introduces his *Politics* with a discussion of the general nature of the *polis*. As often, his treatment of the subject is incomplete; he concentrates on a few aspects of the *polis* and does not attempt to draw his ideas together into an integrated whole. We must try to do this for ourselves by taking the arguments of Book One together with other remarks from the rest of the *Politics* and the *Ethics*. We shall find a set of doctrines about the *polis* which may conveniently be discussed separately but which together form a coherent and impressive theory of the state.

The Political Community

The *Politics*, like many of Aristotle's works, opens with a resounding general statement:

Our own observations tells us that every *polis* is a community of persons formed with a view to some good purpose. I say 'good' because in their actions all men do in fact aim at what they think good. Clearly then, as all communities aim at some good, that one which is supreme and embraces all others will have also as its aim the supreme good. That is the community which we call the *polis* and that type of community we call political.[1]

Aristotle begins his analysis of the *polis* by describing the *polis* as a 'community' (*koinonia*), a concept which is fundamental for his political theory. The noun *koinonia* is derived from the adjective *koinos*, which may refer to anything shared or held in common, and means literally a 'sharing' or 'partnership'. Every *koinonia* is said to be established for some 'good'. By this Aristotle does not mean that every *koinonia* is worthy of his or our approval but only that, in each case, the partners in the *koinonia* are acting together in pursuit of some end or purpose of which they themselves approve. Yet by describing this purpose as 'good', he suggests that communities should properly have morally valuable purposes and that the true *koinonia* will pursue the true good. This illustrates an important feature of Aristotle's theory

---

[1] I.1.i (1252 a 1–7) 25.

of the *polis* that it includes statements about the ideal state as well as about ordinary, imperfect states. This combination of what is and what ought to be, of the descriptive and the evaluative, follows from Aristotle's general philosophical views about the nature of reality and knowledge. All phenomena are to be defined in terms of their 'essence' or essential characteristics which determine both what they really are and what they ought to be. Thus, if 'aiming at good' is an essential characteristic of a *koinonia*, this tells us something both about the definition of a *koinonia* and about what a *koinonia* ought to be like.

Another essential characteristic of any *koinonia* is that it involves, or should involve, both friendship and justice. 'Friendship', a wider concept than in modern English, implies a general sociability, a desire to co-operate in shared activity of any sort, from the utilitarian business transaction to the close, personal relationship of true friends. 'Justice', another fundamental term in Aristotle's ethical and political theory, includes in its broadest sense all the moral principles which should govern people's social behaviour. But it also has more specialized uses referring to particular principles connected with the notion of equality. In politics the most important such principle is distributive justice which governs the distribution of goods and benefits to different members of the same group and it is this aspect of justice which is an essential feature of every *koinonia*. According to distributive justice, each partner's share should be 'equal', not in the sense of 'identical' but in the sense of 'equal to' or 'proportionate to their deserts'. The relative status and therefore deserts of the partners will be different in different communities. In some, for example the community of true friends, the partners will be of equal status and their mutual contributions will be identical. In most, however, the partners will not be strictly equal and they will need to receive different treatment, relative to their respective merits and contributions. In this way distributive justice may be said to 'equalize' the relationship between the partners by distributing benefits in proportion to their deserts. In business relationships the process of equalizing is made easier by the use of units of money which allow the value of different goods to be compared numerically.[2] In other unequal partnerships, such as that of parents and children, there may be no numerical means of comparing the contribution and merits of each partner, but the same principle of proportionate equality will hold. Here the notion of 'equalizing' is not meant

---

[2] *EN* V.5 (1133 b 6–28).

literally; Aristotle knew that one cannot find mathematical precision in such matters. It is used as an analogy for the process of comparing the different deserts of different partners, in the same way as we speak of 'weighing up' or 'balancing' factors which are, strictly speaking, incapable of being balanced or weighed.

There is a limit to the amount of inequality that may obtain between the members of a *koinonia*; there must always be something 'common' between them.[3] What Aristotle means by something 'common' becomes clearer if we look at the type of relationship where it does not exist.[4] The examples he gives are the workman and his tools, the soul and the body, and the master and the slave, all of which are instances of the relation between ends and means. The aims and activities of the body or the slave are wholly subordinate to those of the soul or the master. Thus, to be a full member of a *koinonia* and not just an adjunct to it or someone necessary for its successful operation, a person must share independently in the end or purpose for which the *koinonia* exists. In more modern terms we might say that a member of a *koinonia* must be treated as an 'end in himself'. Aristotle makes considerable use of the distinction between members and subordinates. Though we may object to the way in which he applies the distinction, particularly in relation to slaves, it is one which we still find useful. In an academic community, for example, a tacit distinction is often drawn between those who are full members of the community because they share in the academic purposes for which the community exists and those, such as clerical and domestic staff, who are essential for the existence of the community but are fulfilling a subordinate or ancillary role. For Aristotle another way of describing the status of the full member is to say that he is 'free'. Freedom is essentially a matter of having independent value, of existing for one's own sake and not for another's,[5] rather than of being able to choose and act independently. What distinguishes the slave from the free man, for Aristotle, is not that he is restricted in his actions and subject to coercion but that everything he does is done to serve the interest of someone else.

No English word provides an adequate translation of *koinonia*. Both of the words most frequently used by translators, 'community' and 'association', may be misleading to the student of modern social theory if they suggest the common distinction, based on Tönnies's classification, between community (*Gemeinschaft*) and association (*Gesellschaft*).

---

[3] VII.8.ii (1328 a 25–7) 271.
[4] *EN* VIII.11 (1161 a 34–b 3).   [5] Cf. *Metaphysics* A 2 (982 b 25–6).

In terms of this distinction the typical case of 'community' is the family or the tribe, of 'association' the joint stock company; 'associations' are formed, usually deliberately and contractually, to meet certain specific needs, whereas 'communities' meet a wider set of needs and are cemented by ties of sentiment and sympathy and not just of self-interest. Some of these differences are noticed by Aristotle but they are differences between different types of *koinonia* not between the *koinonia* and some other type of social group. He includes both the strictly utilitarian business partnership and the close-knit family under the heading of *koinonia* and ascribes both the sentiment of friendship or co-operation and the more rational principle of distributive justice to every *koinonia*. Neither 'community' nor 'association' will therefore happily fit every use of *koinonia*, though 'community' is slightly preferable because its etymological connection with 'common' corresponds to the derivation of *koinonia* from *koinos*.

The concept of *koinonia* is useful for social analysis because it identifies certain basic characteristics which are essential to all social groups. It helps to give coherence to Aristotle's theory of the *polis* by placing it within the wider context of general social behaviour and by linking a number of principles which keep recurring, such as the good, justice, and freedom. But the *polis* is more than just a type of *koinonia*; it is a special and unique type.

As all communities aim at some good, that one which is supreme and embraces all others will have also as its aim the supreme good. That is the community which we call the *polis*, and that type of community we call political.[6]

This statement needs to be carefully analysed. First, the *polis* or political community is supreme or most powerful; Aristotle identifies the *polis* with one aspect of the social life of the city-state, the institutions concerned with control over the rest of society. This conception of the political community is similar to the modern notion of the 'state' which is usually defined in terms of the monopoly of legitimate coercion. 'State' is therefore an obviously tempting translation of *polis* and much that Aristotle says of the *polis* can be applied to our state. We should not forget, however, that whereas any independent political community can be called a 'state' the *polis* is a particular type of state. Secondly, the *polis* 'embraces' all the other communities. What does this mean? It might be just another way of saying that the *polis* has

[6] I.1.i (1252 a 3–7) 25.

control over the other communities. But it also suggests that the other communities are included in the *polis* and are therefore parts of the *polis*. As Aristotle says in the *Ethics*, 'all forms of community are like parts of the political community'.[7] In this case Aristotle is considering the *polis* or political community not as one aspect of city-state society but as the whole of that society, including both the controlling, 'political' institutions and the other communities which they control.

This ambiguity between the 'exclusive' and 'inclusive' senses of '*polis*' and 'political community', which sometimes occurs with the modern 'state', affects the validity of Aristotle's conclusion that the *polis* aims at the supreme good. By 'the supreme good', he means complete human good, the good life for all members of the *polis* as distinct from those lesser goods or partial aspects of the good life which are met by the subordinate institutions and communities contained in the *polis*. This view of the purpose of the *polis* is closely connected with the architectonic purpose of political science which he also derives from the fact that the *polis* is the community of supreme power.[8] He believes that the statesman, through the law and other institutions of government, should exercise general control over the citizens in order to make them achieve the good life and that it is the function of political science to instruct the statesman in this task. But this authoritarian view of the role of the state is not, as Aristotle implies, a necessary consequence of defining the state as the institution of supreme authority. Such a definition of the state is compatible with any number of different views about how its authority is to be used and about the extent to which the lives of the citizens should be controlled. Aristotle's illegitimate inference from the supremacy of the state to the conclusion that its function is to use its power without restraint in the pursuit of human good gains plausibility from the ambiguity in his phrase 'embraces all others' and from his failure to distinguish between the inclusive and exclusive senses of '*polis*'. It may be unexceptionable to say that the *polis* aims at total human good if the *polis* is thought to include all aspects of human society. It does not follow from this that the exclusively 'political' institutions of the *polis* should be directly concerned with the achievement of all facets of the good life, many of which may be left completely in the control of other institutions, groups or individuals.

[7] *EN* VIII.9 (1160 ^{a} 8–9).
[8] *EN* I.2 (1094 ^{b} 4–7).

The Polis is Natural

After a brief introduction, Aristotle sets out to prove that the *polis* is natural or exists by nature.[9] This important argument needs to be seen against the background of Greek philosophical debate and of Aristotle's own concept of the natural. He is attempting to answer certain thinkers, including some of the 'sophists', who had claimed that the *polis* and its institutions were contrary to nature. The argument was conducted in terms of the celebrated distinction between *physis* and *nomos*. Both of these words were of wide and elastic meaning: *physis* stood for growth, nature, and fundamental reality; *nomos* for what is man-made, convention, and custom. According to the particular application of the distinction which Aristotle is opposing, men are naturally intent on the pursuit of pleasure and their own advantage at the expense of their fellow men; this is their nature or *physis*. Institutions such as the state and its laws or values such as justice, which encourage men to pursue the common interest and to co-operate rather than compete with one another, are man-made conventions. They are the creations of *nomos*, an inference which was helped by the fact that '*nomos*' was the regular word for law, and opposed to *physis*. From this 'conventionalist' premiss different consequences may be drawn. Law and justice may be rejected and the individual urged to follow his nature, his self-interest, as far as possible. Alternatively, law and justice may be accepted as useful curbs on man's nature, justified by the need to avoid the greater evils which are caused by allowing full rein to his natural impulses. For Aristotle, as for Plato, both of these positions are unacceptable because the premiss itself is unacceptable. Law, justice, and the state, though they owe much to human contrivance, are not to be looked on as evils, even necessary evils, but are to be valued for themselves as things which are fundamentally good and essential for the proper development of human nature. They cannot therefore be contrary to *physis* and the opposition between *nomos* and *physis* must therefore be rejected.

Aristotle sees the natural world as made up of different types or species of object, both animate and inanimate, each with its own distinctive characteristics and capacities. Because this world is constructed according to a coherent and rational pattern, it is proper and generally beneficial that each species should develop and exercise its own natural characteristics. By doing so it realises its 'essence' and performs its work or function. This is its particular good or end (*telos*) which, in Aristotelian language, is both the 'final' and the 'formal' cause of its movement and growth: it is the final cause because it is the end towards which the process of growth is directed; it is the formal cause because it is identified with the 'form' or 'essence' which is realized when a particular thing is fully developed. There are thus a number of interrelated terms all of which depend on the distinctive, natural characteristics of each species: 'nature', 'form', 'essence', 'function', and 'end'. This view of the natural world in which each species has a natural purpose is known as a teleological theory of nature and Aristotle is its most famous exponent. He sometimes sums it up in such phrases as 'nature does nothing without purpose' and 'nature is not niggardly'[10] by which he does not literally mean that nature is a conscious creator but is simply expressing in graphic form his conviction that the world is rational and that each species has natural and distinctive capacities which it ought to develop. In forming this conviction, Aristotle was clearly influenced by his work in biology. The biologist cannot fail to see ordered patterns and processes in the matter he studies. He notices how different species complement each other in a natural balance. He also observes the seed of a tree or the egg of a bird and watches it grow and develop until it is fully formed. That particular seed or egg could not have grown into any other sort of tree or bird and it is easy to assume that it has a particular kind of potentiality within it which it is impelled to realize. When certain instances diverge in some way from the usual pattern the biologist will tend to consider that they would have developed in the 'normal' or 'natural' way if some extraneous factor had not intervened. He will be tempted to say that they have gone 'wrong' and 'ought' to have been allowed to follow their normal and natural course of development. The natural norm has thus become more than an empirical concept; it now carries evaluative overtones about what is best for members of a particular species.

The application of such a theory of nature to human beings and their behaviour raises a familiar difficulty. Assuming that certain characteristics can be identified as natural or innate does it follow that these characteristics ought to be developed rather than restricted? Is this not an unjustifiable inference from what is to what ought to be? We must accept that Aristotle's assumption that the natural is necessarily best and the best necessarily natural is not logically sound. Of anything

---

[10] I.2.x (1253 ᵃ 9) 28; I.2.iii (1252 ᵇ 1–3) 26; I.8.xii (1256·ᵇ 20–1) 40.

natural one may always ask whether it is good or bad and either answer
is logically possible. Yet the attempt to show that certain institutions or
values are based on certain natural characteristics or natural needs is not
therefore completely discredited. The fact, for example, that men
naturally need food and shelter in order to live at least supports the
view, though it may not logically entail it, that they ought to be fed
and housed. Similarly, Aristotle rightly bases his theories of slavery and
the subservience of women on alleged natural differences between slaves
and free and male and female. If we object to these theories it will be
because we think he is wrong about the actual facts of human nature,
not because he has wrongly inferred a value from a fact. The argument
about value will thus turn on a disagreement about fact. In general, we
should not condemn Aristotle for trying to derive political values from
facts about human nature. Instead, we should consider how accurate
his view of human nature is. As we shall see, it can be criticized on the
grounds that it tends to confuse the environmental with the innate and
to assume that behaviour and values that are actually products of Greek
society are universal characteristics of human nature.

Aristotle begins his argument that the *polis* is natural with a sketch
of the development of the *polis* from the household and the village.[11]
He considers the *polis* as if it were a biological organism and tries to
discover its nature by examining the pattern of its growth and development. The first stage is the household which is based on two fundamental distinctions in human nature. One is the difference between
male and female which enables the human race to reproduce itself.
The other is the difference between ruler and ruled, in particular
between the man who has the intellectual capacity for ruling as a
master and the man who can do no more than carry out his master's
orders. These two instinctive relationships, male and female and master
and slave, together with that of parent and child, which is not mentioned
here but is an obvious consequence of the partnership of male and
female, form the household.

The household provides only the simplest necessities and so a number
of households unite into a village which can supply more than men's
daily needs. But the village is still too small and so several villages unite
in a further community, the *polis*, which alone is large enough to be
self-sufficient. The original impetus for this larger community comes
from the need for the necessities of life but it continues to exist for the

---

[11] I.2.i–viii (1252 a 24 – b 34) 26 – 8.

sake of the good life.[12] That is, men first form the *polis* for relatively modest reasons but, once created, it makes possible the realization of more elevated aims which men then come to see as the main reason for its existence. Being self-sufficient the *polis* marks the final stage in a process of natural growth and development; indeed, as it is the final stage, it is itself the 'nature' of human development, the 'essence' which is realized at the end of natural growth.

Therefore the *polis* is a perfectly natural form of community, as the earlier communities from which it sprang were natural. This community is the end of those others and its nature is itself an end; for whatever each thing is when fully grown, that we call its nature, that which man, house, household, or anything else aims at being.[13]

Aristotle clearly intends this argument to be an empirical one, based on observable fact. The household, he believes, is founded on innate biological differences and he gives especial emphasis to the naturalness of the household as if this were the most solid part of the argument, though, as we shall see in the next chapter, his arguments in favour of these innate differences are open to serious objections. He also seems to consider that the sketch of the development of the *polis* from the household is essentially historical; he quotes the historical fact that kingship was the earliest form of government among the Greeks as evidence that the village existed before the *polis* and arose out of the household.[14] Yet even if the account is historically accurate, this does not prove that the development from household to *polis* has universal significance or that it reveals anything about human nature as such. The force of Aristotle's argument must depend not on the mere fact of historical development but on the assumption that the successive human communities of the household, village and *polis* arose to meet certain universal human needs. The *polis* is natural not simply because it is the last stage in an historical evolution but because it alone meets all man's needs; it alone is self-sufficient.

Aristotle refers again to the self-sufficiency of the *polis* in Book Seven when discussing the proper size for the ideal state.[15] He distinguishes two forms of self-sufficiency which correspond to the need for the necessities of life and the need for the good life. Only the *polis* can provide self-sufficiency in both respects. Any community smaller than the *polis* will not be complex enough to provide the variety of

---

[12] Cf. III.6.iii–v (1278 b 20–30) 114;   [13] I.2.viii (1252 b 30–4) 28.
[14] I.2.vi (1252 b 19–22) 27.   [15] VII.4.vii–xiv (1326 a 25–b 25) 265–6.

material goods necessary to maintain life. Aristotle's view of the necessities of life is closely connected with his ethical values. He did not believe that life, in the sense of mere existence, is impossible in a community smaller than the *polis*. When he talks of the necessities of life he must mean the level of material prosperity or external goods which he considers indispensable for the achievement of happiness. On the other hand, any community larger than the *polis* will not provide the good life. Aristotle's preference for the *polis* is not due to ignorance of the existence of other types of state; he is aware of possible alternatives, especially the *ethnos* or nation-state which was often larger than the *polis*. But such states, though large enough to provide the right level of material prosperity, will not be able to offer the good life. Once a community has grown beyond a certain size it cannot be well governed[16] and cannot provide the political participation which every citizen of the ideal *polis* will expect. Within a discussion of the ideal state it is natural that Aristotle should concentrate on the constitutional and political values of the *polis* but his preference for the *polis* extends beyond the specifically political sphere. The whole life of ethical virtue, as described in the *Ethics*, assumes the community of the *polis*. It will involve, for example, meeting one's friends in the *agora* (market-place) or attending the theatre or gymnasium, all of which activities are for Aristotle inextricably connected with the life of the *polis*.

Aristotle's argument that the *polis* is natural because it is self-sufficient and therefore the culmination of a natural process of social evolution thus rests ultimately not on biological or historical fact but on his conception of the good life. Moreover, it rests on that part of his conception of the good life, ethical virtue, which is most closely dependent on the values of his own society and can least plausibly be said to apply to all men as such. Philosophical contemplation can be practised in a variety of different social and political situations. Indeed, in so far as it is a divine activity, it does not require any social relations; a god is self-sufficient and does not require the company of others.[17] It is the ethical virtues and the level of material prosperity necessary for their exercise which tie Aristotle's idea of happiness to the life and culture of the *polis*. His belief that the *polis* is self-sufficient for all men therefore involves attributing an illegitimate universality to the society of the Greek city-state.

---

[16] Cf. III.3.v (1276 a 27–30) 105.
[17] I.2.ix; xiv (1253 a 4; 29) 28; 29.

The importance of the self-sufficiency of the *polis* as evidence for its naturalness is emphasized by a brief subsidiary argument.

Moreover the aim and the end can only be that which is best; and self-sufficiency is both the end and the best.[18]

According to Aristotle's view of nature the natural is best and the best natural. It is therefore open to him to prove the conclusion that the *polis* is natural for man from the premiss that the *polis* is best for man. But though he is willing to use such directly ethical arguments, he does not want to rely on them entirely. In his famous argument that man is a 'political animal', he again tries to found the *polis* on characteristics which are biologically innate.

It follows that the *polis* belongs to a class of objects which exist in nature, and that man is by nature a political animal. He who by his nature and not simply by ill-luck has no *polis* is either too bad or too good, either sub-human or super-human—sub-human like the war-mad man condemned in Homer's words 'having no family, no morals, no home'; for such a person is by his nature mad on war, he is a non-cooperator like an isolated piece in a game of draughts. It is obvious why man is more of a political animal than a bee or any gregarious animal. Nature, as we say, does nothing without some purpose; and for the purpose of making man a political animal she has endowed him alone among the animals with the power of reasoned speech. Speech is something different from voice, which is possessed by other animals also and used by them to express pain or pleasure; for the natural powers of some animals do indeed enable them both to feel pleasure and pain and to communicate these to each other. Speech on the other hand serves to indicate what is useful and what is harmful, and so also what is just and what is unjust.[19]

'Political animal' (*politikon zoon*) literally means 'animal that lives in a *polis*' or '*polis*-animal' and the phrase regularly has this meaning in Aristotle's ethical and political writings. In one of his zoological works, however, he uses the same phrase in a wider sense to refer to any species of animal which co-operates in a common enterprise.[20] The examples he gives, besides man, are bees, wasps, and cranes. In this sense 'political' cannot mean literally 'living in a *polis*', a description which applies only to men, but is closer in meaning to our general word 'social', which implies group activity but does not specify anything about the precise nature of the group. Here, in the *Politics*, Aristotle appears to be deliberately recalling this zoological sense when he says that man is

[18] I.2.ix (1252 b 34–1253 a 1) 28.   [19] I.2.ix–xi (1253 a 1–15) 28.
[20] *Historia Animalium* I.1 (487 b 33–488 a 13).

more of a political animal than bees or any other gregarious animals. By
this cross-reference, he seems to be trying to bring the present argument
into line with the zoological distinction but the attempt is not altogether
successful. If the proposition that man is a 'political' animal is to be
used to prove that the *polis* is natural, 'political' has to be understood
in its literal, not its metaphorical sense; man has to be not merely a
'social' but also a '*polis*' animal. Aristotle distinguishes between man
and other political animals by saying man is 'more political' but, given
the double meaning of 'political', he should more accurately have said
that other animals are 'political' in the metaphorical sense only, whereas
man is also 'political' in the literal sense.

However described, the difference between man and other 'political'
animals is due to man's unique characteristic of *logos,* the capacity for
rationality in thought and speech. Other animals possess the power of
voice or utterance which enables them to express pleasure or pain but
only man also has the capacity for rational speech by which he can
express what is useful and harmful and what is just and unjust.[21] The
'just' is probably to be understood here in its widest sense, covering
social morality. By connecting both usefulness and morality with
logos, Aristotle is opposing those 'conventionalists' who argued that the
pursuit of self-interest was natural but that morality was not and is
claiming instead that both types of behaviour make use of man's
natural biological capacity for rational deliberation and communication.
To separate oneself from moral relations with other people, he argues,
is to deny one's nature. A being which has no natural need for the
society of the *polis* is not a man but either a beast or a god.[22] But
though the pursuit of morality and justice accord with man's natural
characteristics, Aristotle does not have an entirely optimistic view of
human nature as inevitably moral and just. Man's reason enables him
to perceive not only the just but also the unjust; if his morality is
natural, so too is his immorality. Though men have some sort of impulse
which inclines them towards the community of the *polis,* this community is not a spontaneous creation. It has to be deliberately imposed
on men and needs to be reimposed on each succeeding generation.

Among all men, then, there is a natural impulse towards this community; and the first man to build a *polis* deserves credit for conferring
very great benefits. As man is the best of all animals when he has

[21] Cf. VII.13.xii (1332 b 3–5) 284.
[22] I.2.xiv (1253 a 29) 29.

reached his full development, so he is worst of all when divorced from law and justice.[23]

Man is therefore a *polis*-animal also in the sense that, if he is to realize his moral potential, he needs the order and control which are provided by the government of the *polis*; the moral perfection of the members of the *polis* can be achieved only by means of publicly administered law.

The argument that man is a 'political animal', with its references to other animals and to man's natural characteristics, is intended to base the naturalness of the *polis* on biological fact. But, though Aristotle may have provided evidence for the social nature of man and for man's need for a coercive state, he has not shown that this society and state must be of the *polis* type. Social relations and morality are possible in states of different types, for example the nation-state or *ethnos*. To establish the superior claims of the *polis* over other types of state, Aristotle must rely again on his conception of the good life and of man's natural needs. He probably understands the justice which he connects with man's natural faculty of *logos* not as any unspecified social morality but rather as his particular conception of ethical virtue which is closely associated with the *polis*. The argument that man is a 'political animal' closely follows, and is supported by, the argument that only the *polis* is self-sufficient. The attempt to prove that the *polis* is natural thus depends once again on Aristotle's view of the good life and is again open to the objection that it makes unwarranted claims of biological universality for values which are, at least in part, peculiar to one particular social context.

Aristotle's view of the role of the *polis* in making men moral is also open to criticism. He seems to assume that because the *polis* is self-sufficient for the good life, the aim of the statesman and the laws must be to make men good. He develops this argument most fully in Book Three while attempting to refute the view that the state is concerned solely with preventing citizens from doing harm to one another or from breaking their agreements.[24] This conception of the state, which Aristotle attributes to the sophist Lycophron, is essentially similar to the 'minimal' state of modern liberalism. It reduces the state, in Aristotle's opinion, to 'a mere alliance'. It is mistaken because it misconceives the proper purpose of the *polis* which is not just the prevention of mutual crime and the promotion of economic exchange but also the provision

[23] I.2.xv (1253 ª 29–33) 29.
[24] III.9.vi–viii (1280 ª 31–b 12) 119–20.

of the good life in a self-sufficient community.[25] Aristotle's argument is fallacious and depends on the ambiguity between the 'exclusive' and 'inclusive' senses of *polis* which led to a similar fallacy about the all-embracing aim of the political community. On the one hand, *polis* refers exclusively to one particular aspect of the city-state, the specifically political institutions in contrast to other institutions and groups, such as families, business partnerships, and so on; it is the political community as distinct from all the other communities. On the other hand, *polis* may mean the whole society, including all these other communities. It is in the latter, inclusive sense that man is a *polis*-animal and that the *polis* is self-sufficient for the good life; the good life is lived not just within the institutions of government (indeed political participation is dispensable) but also, and to a much greater extent, within the family and groups of friends. It is the former, exclusive sense, however, which has to be understood when Aristotle says that the *polis* must bring about human perfection through the agency of the statesman and the law. Once this ambiguity has been revealed it becomes clear that acceptance of the moral value and purpose of the *polis* does not imply that the government should exercise total control over the moral welfare of its subjects. Aristotle's authoritarianism, however, is not simply the result of fallacious argument. Its roots, as we shall see, run much deeper, in his belief in objective values, in his faith in the powers of education and law and in a conception of freedom which emphasizes correctness rather than autonomy of action. These convictions which support his authoritarianism help him to overlook weaknesses in his attempts to justify it.

Two major criticisms of Aristotle's arguments have emerged. First and most important, his attempt to show that the *polis* and only the *polis* accords with man's innate characteristics and meets essentially human needs is unsuccessful. The arguments ultimately depend not on biological fact but on his own moral convictions which are not shown to be universally valid for all human beings. Secondly, he makes an illegitimate inference about the role of government and law from his view of the purpose of the *polis*. But in spite of these objections, there is still much of value in what he says. If we look beyond his emphasis on the *polis* and his assumption that it is the best form of community, we shall find that his arguments have important implications for social and political theory. In particular, he makes some good points not only

[25]   III.9.xii (1280 [b] 29–35) 120.

against his 'conventionalist' opponents, who also argued within the
context of the *polis*, but against all whose theories of morality and the
state depend on seeing human beings as 'atomized' and self-interested
individualists. Assuming that rationality, including the ability to deliberate and choose, is man's most important distinguishing feature, an
assumption that would still find wide support, it makes good sense to
argue that morality is no less natural than the calculated pursuit of self-
interest; both employ, and are impossible without, man's reasoning
capacity. Moreover, the view that rationality is essentially social and
cannot be developed except in the company of others is one that is
accepted by many modern philosophers who see the social phenomenon
of language as the basis of reasoning and thought. Aristotle, it is true,
does not go so far as to derive all the internal or 'mental' aspects of
rationality from the public activity of speaking, but his recognition that
rationality is at least in part a social activity is important because it
shows that men, if naturally rational, are also naturally social. He also
perceives that men desire society for its own sake, quite apart from any
personal benefits that it may bring. He does not mean to deny that
society confers advantages, but he does deny that this is the only reason
why men live together. As he says in Book Three, when recalling the
argument that man is a 'political animal',

Men have a natural desire for life in society, even when they have no
need to seek each other's help.[26]

Furthermore, he recognizes the dynamic nature of the relation between
individuals and their social institutions when he says that the *polis*
began from the need for life but continued in existence because of the
need for the good life. He is prepared to concede to the 'conventionalists'
that the origin of the *polis* may lie in the desire for material advantage
and that it may have been looked on at first as a necessary evil. But he
does not argue that this is the only reason why men who have been
brought up in the *polis* value the life of their community. He understands how institutions may be founded for certain purposes but may
subsequently create opportunities for new and unforeseen activities
which alter their original *raison d'être*.

   In general, then, Aristotle may be said to have had the better of the
argument with his 'conventionalist' opponents. At the same time he
does not go too far in the opposite direction. Though he rejects the

[26]   III.6.iii (1278 ^{b} 20–1) 114.

view that men are naturally individualistic and self-interested, he does not believe that they are naturally so social that they can co-operate spontaneously without any external coercion. He is certainly no anarchist; indeed, he places excessive reliance on authoritarian control. If we approach it in this way, ignoring those aspects which are inextricably tied to the Greek city-state, Aristotle's doctrine that the *polis* is natural yields a view of human beings as creatures who naturally enjoy and benefit from living together in society but who cannot be relied on to live harmoniously without the coercive institution of the state. Every general theory of the state, of its purposes and of its relation to its subjects, must be founded on some such general view of human nature and human needs. The one we can abstract from Aristotle may not be completely convincing but it is certainly more plausible than many that have been offered in the history of political thought.

The Whole and its Parts

Aristotle also regards the *polis* as a 'compounded whole'. The main function of this doctrine is to unite and give theoretical coherence to a number of different features of the *polis*, most of which are described elsewhere in less technical language. Aristotle makes a general distinction between groups which are 'wholes' and those which are mere 'aggregates' or 'heaps'.[27] Mere aggregates possess a certain unity but only because their parts are juxtaposed. 'Wholes', on the other hand, have parts which are unified not just by their contiguity but also by something else; they share a unity of 'form'. For example, the parts of a shoe, if put together in a random fashion, may have the unity of an aggregate, but only when they are combined in a shoe will they make up a whole because only then will they have a single form. Thus when Aristotle describes the *polis* as a whole[28] he means that its members are not 'atomized' individuals related to one another only by the fact that they inhabit the same territory; they share in the joint activity of a *koinonia* which gives a form or unity to the group as a whole. Calling the *polis* a 'whole' is therefore another way of saying that it is a *koinonia*.

The unity of the *polis*, however, is not so great that the parts are completely lost in the whole. The *polis* is not a 'mixture' or a 'blending' like a solution of honey and water in which the texture is uniform throughout; it is a 'compound' in which the original parts are still

---

[27] *Metaphysics* Δ6 (1016 ^{b} 11–17); Z 17 (1041 ^{b} 11–19).
[28] e.g. I.2.xiii (1253 ^{a} 20) 29; III.1.ii (1274 ^{b} 38–40) 102; VII.8.i (1328 ^{a} 21–5) 271.

discernible.[29] This implies that the *polis* is made up of different people and groups performing different but complementary functions. In criticizing Plato's proposal to abolish the family, Aristotle objects to the assumption, which he thinks Plato is making, that the greater the unity of the *polis* the better.[30] The *polis* is a plurality composed of dissimilar parts with differing though mutually complementary functions. The attempt to remove this diversity by making the parts similar will destroy the self-sufficiency of the *polis* and therefore the *polis* itself.[31] This argument, it should be noted, hardly counts against the *Republic*, the whole structure of which depends on a rigid division of labour. The unity that Aristotle criticizes occurs only within the ruling class and not in the *polis* as a whole. Moreover, even within this class, Plato does not mean to destroy all differentiation but only that which he thinks will lessen the solidarity of its members. As usual when dealing with the ideas of his predecessors, Aristotle is not concerned to interpret them accurately and sympathetically but simply uses them as a starting-point for developing his own arguments. In his treatment of Plato we can also sometimes detect an attitude of niggling criticism, a desire to find fault and to exaggerate the differences between his own political theory and that of his former teacher.

The extent of the diversity which Aristotle considers essential to the existence and survival of the *polis* should not be exaggerated. His argument has sometimes been interpreted as evidence of a 'pluralist' view that all political communities necessarily consist of different groups with different and conflicting interests and that politics is necessarily concerned with the reconciliation of these interests. Though he recognizes that most ordinary states will have to accommodate such differences, this is not part of his general theory of the *polis* because it does not apply to the ideal state. Ideally, the individual citizens, though they perform different functions, will be united in the pursuit of a common ideal of happiness.[32] Diversity of function does not necessarily imply diversity of values or interests. Thus Aristotle does not agree with the pluralist that the members of a political community will always have conflicting views about the public good; though he opposes Plato's abolition of the family and private property he does not reject the Platonic ideal of an ethically united community.

[29] e.g. I.1.iii (1252 ^{a} 18–21) 25; III.1.ii (1274 ^{b} 38–40) 102.
[30] II.2.ii (1261 ^{a} 15–22) 56.
[31] II.2.viii (1261 ^{b} 10–15) 57–8.
[32] Cf. VIII.1; I.13.xv (1260 ^{b} 13–18) 53–4; V.9.xi–xii (1310 ^{a} 12–19) 215–16.

Aristotle divides the *polis* into more than one set of parts. In Book One it is lesser communities like the household and the village which are related to the *polis* as parts to the whole. But when Aristotle talks of the diversity of the different parts of the *polis*, he has in mind different occupational functions such as farming, warfare, deliberation, and adjudication.[33] Again, when he is discussing the nature of citizenship, it is the individual citizens who are the basic parts of the *polis*.[34] There is no need to see these differences as contradictions; they simply show that the doctrine of the whole and its parts is a flexible explanatory device. Like a modern political scientist Aristotle varies the classifications he uses to fit the particular questions he is asking. But there are limits to this flexibility. A part is to be distinguished from something 'without which not', that is a necessary condition or *sine qua non*. Many things may be necessary for the existence of a whole, but they are not therefore parts of it. To be a true part of a whole, an element must share in the form or purpose for which the whole exists. In the case of a whole made up of human parts, there is an exact parallel with the theory of the *koinonia*, whereby people are true members of a *koinonia* only if they share in its common end or purpose. The end for which the *polis* exists is the good life and anybody who shares in this end may be described as a part. Lesser communities, such as the household, qualify as parts because the ends which they pursue, though limited, are part of the common end of happiness pursued by the *polis*. Similarly, citizens are parts because they share in the constitution which incorporates the aim of a *polis* while people such as slaves or foreigners are not parts of the *polis* but merely necessary conditions.[35] Finally, certain functions may properly be termed parts because they are essential activities of the citizen and therefore components of the city's well-being.[36]

The best-known and most easily misunderstood aspect of the doctrine that the *polis* is a whole is Aristotle's argument that the whole is prior to its parts and therefore that the *polis* is prior to the individual. It occurs in Book One as part of the argument that man is a 'political animal'.

Furthermore the *polis* has priority over the household and over any individual among us. For the whole must be prior to the parts. Separate

---

[33] IV.4.ix–xvii (1290 ^{b} 38–1291 ^{b} 2) 156–8; VII.8.vi–ix (1328 ^{b} 2–23) 272.

[34] III.1.ii (1274 ^{b} 41) 102.   [35] III.5.i–iv (1277 ^{b} 34–1278 ^{a} 15) 111.

[36] IV.4.xiv (1291 ^{a} 24–7) 157; VII.9.iv (1329 ^{a} 2–5) 273.

hand or foot from the whole body and they will no longer be hand or foot (except in name, as one might speak of a hand or foot sculptured in stone). It will have been ruined by such treatment, having no longer the power and the function which make it what is is. So, though we may use the same words, we cannot say that we are speaking of the same thing. It is clear then that the *polis* is both natural and prior to the individual. For as an individual is not fully self-sufficient after separation, he will stand in the same relationship to the whole as the other parts. Whatever is incapable of participating in the community which we call the *polis*, a dumb animal for example, and equally whatever is perfectly self-sufficient and needs nothing from the *polis* (e.g. a god), these are not parts of the *polis* at all.[37]

What does Aristotle mean when he says that the whole is prior to its parts, that the *polis* is prior to the household and the individual? Apart from its ordinary, temporal sense of 'coming before', 'prior' has two more specialized senses in Aristotle. First, 'what is posterior in the order of becoming is prior in the order of nature.'[38] This is a clear reference to the teleological theory of nature. Any process of natural growth and development is directed towards some goal or end; this goal, the full realization of a thing's nature, is presupposed during the whole process of growth and knowledge of it is necessary for understanding and explaining this process. The end is in this sense 'prior' to the beginning. Secondly, 'a thing is said to be prior to other things when, if it does not exist, the others will not exist, whereas it can exist without the others.'[39] The *polis* is prior in both of these specialized senses. The account of the development of the *polis* from the household and the village has established that the *polis* is posterior in the order of becoming, but prior in the order of nature, because it is the end towards which man's social development is directed. In the passage quoted, Aristotle is arguing that the *polis* is also prior in the second sense. The *polis* can exist without the individual but the individual cannot exist without the *polis*. He does not mean that the *polis* can actually exist without any individuals as parts though it can withstand the loss of any particular individual. The main point is that the individual cannot exist without the *polis*. If men are separated from the *polis*, they cease to be men in the same way as a hand ceases to be a hand if cut off from the body. We still refer to such severed hands as 'hands' but the meaning of the word has changed. The reason why the meaning has changed is that, for Aristotle, the definition or meaning of a word identifies its essence or

---

[37] I.2.xii–xiv (1253 ^{a} 18–29) 29..   [38] *Physics* VIII.7 (261 ^{a} 13–15).
[39] *Physics* VIII.7 (260 ^{b} 17–19).

the function that it should properly perform. The severed hand is no longer able to perform its function once it is separated from the body and so ceases to be a 'hand'. Similarly, the function of man, the realization of his essence, lies in the achievement of the good life which, as we have seen, cannot be lived except in the *polis*. Therefore, anyone who lives outside the *polis* has ceased to exist as a 'man'.

The argument that the *polis* is prior is therefore nothing more than a restatement in more technical language of Aristotle's doctrine, based on his conception of happiness, that the *polis* is natural. It adds nothing substantially new but is rather a piece of theoretical consolidation in which he relates his account of the *polis* to some of his other philosophical doctrines about priority and definition. Unfortunately, the argument is sometimes quoted out of context and without proper understanding of the technical terms involved. It has figured prominently in two interpretations of Aristotle's theory of the *polis* which deserve further consideration: that he subordinates the individual to the state and that he adopts an 'organic' theory of the state.

The question whether Aristotle subordinates the individual to the state cannot be simply answered because the notion of subordination of individual to state is itself not a simple one. In one sense it may refer to the priority of ends or purposes. The state may be said to be subordinated to the individual if the purpose of the state is restricted to the pursuit of individual aims, for example the protection from physical harm, which can be described without any reference to the state and are therefore logically prior to the notion of the state. Conversely, the individual is subordinated to the state if the activities of the individual are confined to the pursuit of collective goals, such as national wealth and glory, the description of which contains reference to the state. These are both extreme positions and many views of the relation between individual and state lie between them. The individual may pursue both national and personal goals; the state may aim at both public and private benefits for its citizens. In such intermediate cases, neither the purpose of the state nor those of the individual are subordinate to each other. Aristotle's theory falls into this middle category. The *polis* achieves its purpose when its citizens are happy, and they are happy when living the life of intellectual and ethical virtue. Ethical virtue involves relations with others but it is not primarily concerned with specifically public or political activity. It may involve the exercise of political power but it also extends through all the other social communities such as the household and the partnerships of friends. The lives of Aristotle's citizens, therefore, cannot be said to be wholly swallowed up in service to the state. Such a view involves a confusion of the inclusive and exclusive senses of *polis*. The good life may be wholly lived in the *polis* in the inclusive sense but this does not mean that men's lives are wholly involved in the *polis* in the exclusive sense of 'state' or 'political institutions'. At the same time, Aristotle is not wholly an individualist. The good life does not categorically exclude all reference to the state, and Aristotle appears to value some specifically national goals, such as peace and prosperity for the city, for their own sake and not just as means towards individual happiness.[40] In this sense, then, Aristotle cannot be said to have subordinated the individual to the state, or the state to the individual.

Though the individual member of the *polis* is not completely devoted to the service of the state, it is true, however, that the good of any individual member is less important than the good of the whole. Aristotle's political theory is written from the point of view of the ruler rather than the subject and he is more concerned with the community as a whole than with the fate of particular individuals.[41] Like all ancient Greeks, he has little conception of individual or human rights, of obligations which are due to all individuals because they are individual human beings. In comparison with ourselves who have been brought up in a tradition which respects the rights of the individual, the Greeks were much more willing to sacrifice the status, property, or lives of individuals for the sake of the common good. Because the individual had no inherent rights, there was less sense of conflict between competing claims of individual and state and therefore less sense of sacrifice in depriving individuals of their property or liberties. In this respect we may say that Aristotle subordinates the individual to the state if we mean that in balancing the claims of individual and state, he favours the state more, and the individual less, than we would find acceptable. But we should remember that this is true not only of authoritarian Greek writers like Plato and Aristotle but also of the more liberal supporters of democracy. The democratic institution of ostracism by which individuals could be banished without being convicted of any formal charge provides a good example of the general Greek view of the legitimate power of the group over the individual.

There is another, closely related sense in which Aristotle may also be said to subordinate the individual to the state. This concerns not ends

---

[40] VII.2.
[41] Cf. III.13.xx–xxi (1284 ^{b} 3–13) 133–4.

or purposes but the means by which these purposes are achieved. The individual is subordinated to the state if the state assumes total authority for the achievement of the individual's goals and does not allow the individual any freedom to pursue his own goals according to his own choice. (In this sense there is no intelligible converse position of the state being wholly subordinate to the individual; it would imply that the state had no authority over individuals, in which case there would be no state at all.) This type of subordination of individual to state, which may also be described as 'totalitarian', 'authoritarian', or 'paternalistic', is certainly endorsed by Aristotle. He considers that the best way to make people happy is through legislation and state-controlled education and he places little value on individual freedom in the sense of personal autonomy or the right to act as one chooses. The question of the relation between individual and state in Aristotle is thus not a simple one and needs to be answered by looking at the whole of his political theory and not by concentrating on a few remarks taken out of context.

Aristotle is also said to have advanced the, or an, 'organic' theory of the state. The phrase 'organic theory' or any close equivalent does not actually occur in Aristotle's text, but this would not be a serious objection to calling Aristotle's theory 'organic' if to do so were to make his meaning clearer. In general terms, an organic theory is one which explains the political community by comparing it with a living organism and we must certainly admit the undoubted influence of biological ways of thinking on Aristotle's ethical and political writings and that biological and medical examples abound in them. However, the description 'organic', often contrasted with 'mechanical', also has several more precise meanings which are derived from particular biological analogies.

First, the political community, like the living organism, contains a number of parts which perform different but complementary functions which contribute to the survival and well-being of the whole. This doctrine is certainly held by Aristotle who several times insists on the differentiation of the parts of the *polis* but it is common to most theories of the state including so-called 'mechanical' theories. It really involves no more than a recognition of the need for some sort of division of labour in a complex society. Secondly, the distinction between 'organic' and 'mechanical' conceptions of the state is sometimes similar to the distinction between 'community' and 'association' mentioned earlier. Aristotle's *polis* is a 'community' rather than an 'association', because men value it for its own sake and not just as means to the fulfilment of separate, individual ends. In this sense, too, his theory may be called 'organic'.

Thirdly, the description 'organic' may sometimes be applied to a particular conception of historical development which is contrasted with the 'rationalist' belief in the possibility of wholesale, root-and-branch reform. There are two forms of this organic argument, which may be called the weak and the strong theses. The weak thesis is that completely radical change is impossible because we can never have a clean slate on which to start. Human beings will always be to some extent determined by their previous historical situation and their capacity for change will always be correspondingly limited. The strong thesis, on the other hand, is an unjustifiable inference from this valid premiss to the false conclusion that all attempts at deliberate change are impossible or undesirable. Aristotle is certainly conservative in his attitude to change. He is opposed to frequent changes in the law[42] and is aware of the general effects of education and tradition on political institutions. But he combines conservative political principles with a belief in the possibility, if only remote, of constructing an ideal state from scratch. He is not very interested in utopias but he is not anti-utopian on principle. In this sense, then, his theory is not organic.

Finally, the view which is perhaps most commonly called 'organic' is that the sole purpose of the members of a community, like the organs of a living organism, is to serve the collective interest of the state which is prior to, or more real than, its constituent parts. This is how the organic theory has usually been represented by its hostile critics. To attribute such a theory to Aristotle, as we have seen, is to misunderstand his view of the relation of the individual to the state and his doctrine that the whole is prior to its parts. Thus, in some respects, Aristotle's political theory may be called 'organic'. But, because of the variety of meanings of 'organic' and because some supposedly 'organic' doctrines are not endorsed by him, it is not at all helpful to use this term as an aid, let alone the key, to understanding Aristotle's theory of the *polis*.

The Types of Rule

One of the implications for Aristotle of the doctrine that the *polis* is a compounded whole is that every *polis* will contain the process of ruling, involving both a ruler and a subject.[43] He sees the relation of hierarchy, of superior and subordinate, throughout the natural world

[42] II.8. xxiii–xxiv (1269 ^{a} 13–24) 82–3.
[43] I.5.iii (1254 ^{a} 28–32) 33.

but it is of particular significance for political science. The political community is defined in terms of its control over all other communities and politics is therefore essentially concerned with the exercise of power. The nature of the process of ruling provides the first problem in the study of politics. In the first chapter of Book One Aristotle criticizes the commonly held view that statesmen, kings, heads of households, and masters of slaves all rule in the same way.[44] This, he believes is a misconception; there are qualitative as well as quantitative differences between the different types of rule which will be of fundamental importance for political theory. The nature of these qualitative differences is one of the subsidiary themes of Book One and serves to connect the lengthy examination of the household with the general theory of the *polis*.

The modern political scientist would probably want to distinguish different types of rule in terms of differences in political institutions or in the techniques of decision-making. For Aristotle, however, the most important difference lies in the aims and intentions with which power is exercised. His basic distinction is between 'free' and 'despotic' rule. The nature of free rule follows from his conception of freedom. To be free is to have independent value, to exist for one's own sake and not for another's. Free rule is therefore rule in which the interests of the subject are pursued by the ruler. There is no contradiction between being ruled and being free, because freedom is connected not with independence of action but with independence of value. The opposite of free rule is despotic rule. 'Despotic' literally means 'like the master of a slave' (*despotes*) but despotic rule is not restricted to the relationship of master and slave. It refers to any type of rule where the ruler rules not in his subjects' but in his own interests. The distinction between free and despotic rule is not necessarily a distinction between good and bad rule; there are some people, according to Aristotle, who deserve to be ruled despotically.

Aristotle makes a further distinction within free rule between kingly and political rule.[45] Kingly rule is the rule of superior over inferior whereas political rule is of equals over equals. Political rule typically involves the alternation of rulers and ruled; because none have superior qualifications which would justify their being made permanent leaders, the only fair method is to share power or take turn and turn about.[46]

---

[44] I.1.ii (1252 ^{a} 7–16) 25.
[45] I.7.i (1255 ^{b} 18–20) 37; I.12.i–ii (1259 ^{a} 37–b 6) 49–50.
[46] II.2.vi–vii (1261 ^{a} 37–b 6) 57.

Aristotle's statement in the *Ethics* that political justice is found among men who are 'free and either proportionately or arithmetically equal'[47] implies that the qualifications of those who share in political rule need not be absolutely equal. Fitness for leadership may vary from person to person and some will deserve to be given a greater share in ruling than others. If proportionate equality is allowed, each person must merely have *some* claim entitling him to *some* share in ruling. This is still sufficient to distinguish 'political' from 'kingly' rule, for in kingly rule the subjects have no share in ruling at all. Aristotle thus distinguishes three general types of rule: despotic, kingly, and political. This classification will prove useful in the analysis of constitutions but its immediate purpose, as we shall see, is to illuminate the different relationships in the household.

[47] *EN* V.6 (1134 a 26−8).

CHAPTER THREE

THE HOUSEHOLD

Of the two lesser communities, the household and the village, which are parts of the *polis* and precede it in time, the household is much more important in Aristotle's ethical and political theory. Though the village provides a necessary link between the household and the *polis* in the chain of historical development, Aristotle ignores it as an integral part of the fully developed *polis*. The household, on the other hand, continues to have important functions. Its origins lie in the instincts of reproduction and self-preservation and in the need to provide the basic necessities of life and it remains, as it was in Greek society of Aristotle's time, the institution which provides for the procreation and rearing of children and which produces much of the economic wealth of the *polis*. Once it has become part of the *polis*, the household is also closely involved in the aims of the larger community. It is very important as an educational institution, introducing children into the morality of the community. It is, moreover, the centre of life for over half the population of the city, that is for women, children, and slaves. Plato, realizing the moral influence of the household and fearing that it would conflict with, and undermine, the public-spiritedness of the rulers, had advocated in the *Republic* the abolition of the household for the ruling class. Wives were to be held in common and there was to be no private property. He hoped to remove the conflict between public and private interest by the simple, if highly radical, device of removing private interest altogether. Aristotle disagrees with these proposals very strongly and his criticism of the *Republic* in Book Two[1] is largely taken up with objections to the community of wives and property. Many of his arguments are now part of the stock-in-trade of conservative opposition to communism. For example, disputes about property are due not to the existence of private property but to human wickedness. (In fairness to Plato, however, we should remember that Plato considers communism to be only part of the solution; moral education will also be necessary.) Indeed, sharing property may even lead to an increase in disputes.[2] More generally, Aristotle considers that people will not extend to the wives, children, and property held in common the same feelings of possession and affec-

[1] II.1–5. [2] II.5.xii (1263 b 22–7) 64–5.

tion that they have held for their personal family and property.[3] Communism, in short, is contrary to human nature.

Moreover there is an immense amount of pleasure to be derived from the sense of ownership; every man bears love towards himself and I am sure that nature meant this to be so.[4]

Communism of families and property also destroys the possibility of exercising certain ethical virtues, for example temperance towards other men's wives and personal generosity and liberality.[5] Similarly, abolition of the family will cause problems in relation to such immoral acts as incest and parricide.[6] Arguments of this sort may seem to beg the question; they assume the existence of values essentially connected with the household and then claim that these values will be destroyed if the household is destroyed. The radical might reasonably reply that when the household is destroyed there will be no more need for these values. But it is typical of Aristotle's approach that he should be unwilling to depart too far from the experience and values of the society in which he lived. Like the *polis*, the household was too deeply entrenched in the social life of the Greeks for him to be able to accept its abolition.

Though Aristotle rejects Plato's communism, he does not dismiss the problem which Plato was trying to solve. He recognizes that the private interests of the household and its members may clash with the interests of the *polis* as a whole. Hence the importance which he attaches to the household as an institution of moral education and his belief that the organization of the household is a matter of vital public concern and therefore a proper part of the subject matter of political science.

Every household is part of a *polis*; and the virtue of the part ought to be examined in relation to the virtue of the whole. This means that children, and women too, must be educated with an eye to the whole constitution of the *polis*—at least if it is true to say that it makes a difference to the goodness of a state that its children should be good and its women good. And it must make a difference; for women make up half the adult free population and from children come those who will participate in the constitution.[7]

The pivotal figure is the head of the household who acts as a link. between the political community and the smaller community of the household. He will typically be a citizen and therefore a full member of

[3] II.3.iv–ix (1261 ^{b} 32–1262 ^{a} 24) 58–9; II.5.vi (1263 ^{a} 27–9) 63.
[4] II.5.viii (1263 ^{a} 40–b 1) 63–4.   [5] II.5.x (1263 ^{b} 7–14) 64.
[6] II.4.i–iii (1262 ^{a} 25–40) 60.   [7] I.13.xv–xvi (1260 ^{b} 13–20) 53–4.

the *polis* and will also be in charge of the other members of his house-hold as well as of the family property. Control of the other members of the household will be exercised through the three household relation-ships of husband and wife, father and children, master and slave. Each of these relationships includes the head of the household as ruler but each involves a different type of rule.

Slavery

The relationship of master and slave is discussed at some length in the first book of the *Politics*.[8] Aristotle's account of slavery seems to us to be one of the weakest parts of his political theory, not just because a defence of slavery is offensive to modern sensibilities, but because the arguments he offers are particularly inconsistent and unconvincing. He begins by offering a definition of a slave.[9] A slave is one of the 'instru-ments' or 'tools' necessary for the existence of the household and is part of the master's property. He is an instrument of action rather than of production; unlike the craftsman he does not help in the creation of a product but rather assists his master in the business of living. As the slave is an instrument or means serving the ends of his master it follows that he has no interest of his own apart from his master's.[10] He is thus, according to Aristotle's concept of freedom, 'unfree' because he has no independent value. The rule of master (*despotes*) over slave is the paradigm case of 'despotic' rule, the type of rule which is exercised solely in the interests of the ruler.

As a definition of the status of the slave, particularly the domestic slave, this is ruthless but reasonably accurate. But as well as describing the relation between master and slave, Aristotle also wants to prove that slavery is justified because it is based on natural differences. The distinction between *nomos* and *physis* had been applied to the institu-tion of slavery as well as the *polis* as a whole with the implication that there was no natural or innate difference between slave and master and that the institution of slavery was based wholly on convention (*nomos*). What made a man a slave was simply the fact that he had been captured in war or born of slave parents and was classed as a slave by the law of the land. For Aristotle this fact alone cannot provide a valid justification for treating a man as a slave; to say that a man deserves to be a slave simply because the law says he is a slave amounts to equating justice with the rule of the stronger or might with right.[11] If slavery is to be

---

[8] I.4–7; 13.   [9] I.4.
[10] Cf. III.6.vi (1278 b 32–7) 114.   [11] I.6.iv (1255 a 17–18) 35.

acceptable, there must be people whose natural capacities fit them for being slaves; for only if something is naturally fitted to perform a particular function is it best for it to perform this function. To justify slavery Aristotle must therefore identify the characteristics of the natural slave which fit him for slavery. He does not believe that all people who are actually held as slaves are natural slaves. He distinguishes between natural slaves and slaves in law and recognizes that having been captured in war does not prove that a person is naturally fitted for slavery.[12] He is simply arguing that there are some people somewhere who are natural slaves and it is in support of this argument that he quotes the common belief, which he himself endorses, that barbarians, or non-Greeks, are naturally servile.[13]

The natural slave is usually distinguished, he says, by a difference of physique. The slave should have strength to perform his duties but should not have the upright stature which is best suited for the military and political life of the citizen.[14] This difference, however, is of secondary importance only. The principal criterion of the natural slave is mental or psychological not physical. Though nature 'intends' to match external and internal characteristics, she is not always successful; free minds sometimes exist in servile bodies and *vice versa*. It is thus impossible to recognize a slave from his physical appearance alone; one must also examine the nature of his mind or soul.

At first Aristotle seems to deny the slave any share in the rational faculty (*logos*) which is the distinctive feature of human beings. The natural slave, we are told, differs from his master in the same way as the body differs from the soul or animals from men;[15] he is a separable part of his master's body, ruled by his master's soul in the same way as the master rules his own body. But Aristotle quickly qualifies this position. Though the slave may be used as if he were an extension of his master's body or an animal, it would be clearly absurd to say that slaves are no more rational than other animals. Instead, Aristotle says that though the slave does not possess full reason he can apprehend what is rational. In this respect the slave is different from other animals which cannot apprehend language but merely follow their instincts.[16] This account of the slave's mentality is to be understood within the context of the psychological theory of the *Ethics*. There Aristotle distinguishes between

[12] I.6.ix (1255 b 4–5) 36.
[13] I.6.vi–vii (1255 a 28–38) 36; cf. I.2.iv (1252 b 5–9) 26–7.
[14] I.5.x (1254 b 25–32) 34.   [15] I.5.viii (1254 b 16–20) 33–4.
[16] I.5.ix (1254 b 20–4) 34.

two rational pairs of the soul (*psyche*), that which deliberates and controls and that which feels and desires and can apprehend and obey reason.[17] The slave has the latter part but not the former; though he may be said to have some share in reason, he does not possess full reason because he is without the controlling elements.

This is the account of the psychology of the slave on which Aristotle bases his argument that there are people for whom slavery is naturally justified. In several places, however, he is forced to admit that the behaviour both of slaves and of their masters towards them implies that the slave is not completely lacking in the capacity to deliberate and act rationally. For example he says that the slave should have some share in the ethical virtues of courage and self-control, sufficient at least to perform his work properly.[18] If the slave can be expected to act virtuously even to this extent, he must be capable of independent action and not confined to blind obedience to his master's orders. The inconsistency is most striking in Aristotle's attitude to the possibility of friendship between a master and a slave. Friendship and partnership in a *koinonia* involve relations of reciprocity and proportional justice which cannot, by definition, exist between people related only as means and end. Sometimes, therefore, Aristotle denies the possibility of friendship between them because there can be no justice or *koinonia*.[19] At other times, however, he allows the possibility of such friendship and distinguishes between a master-and-slave relationship which is based on friendship and one which is based simply on coercion.[20] In the *Ethics* he tries to resolve the difficulty by saying that one cannot be friends with a slave *qua* slave but one can be friends with him *qua* man.[21] But this merely emphasizes the confusion in the argument. If it is justifiable to treat the slave as a man how is it at the same time justifiable to rule him as a slave? The justification of slavery depends on seeing the slave as lacking full reason and therefore not really human while friendship implies seeing him as an equal, as another man. By thus admitting the possibility of friendship with natural slaves, Aristotle himself disproves the existence of a class of 'subhuman men' on whose existence the whole theory of natural slavery depends.

Furthermore, even if Aristotle could have found men with no deliberative reason but only the ability to understand commands, it would be

---

[17] *EN* 1.13 (1102 ^{b} 13–1103 ^{a} 3).
[18] I.13.xii (1260 ^{a} 33–6) 52–3; cf. I.13.ii–iii (1259 ^{b} 21–8) 51.
[19] *EN* VIII.11 (1161 ^{a} 32–b 3).
[20] I.6.x (1255 ^{b} 12–15) 37.
[21] *EN* VIII.11 (1161 ^{b} 5–8).

inconsistent with his own doctrines to treat such people wholly as means with no independent value of their own. He introduces his account of natural slavery with a description of different types of rule within the individual person.

The rule of soul over body is despotic, the rule of intellect over desire is political and kingly.[22]

According to this analogy, despotic rule or slavery is justified when there is such a difference between ruler and ruled as exists between soul and body. However, once Aristotle stops seeing the slave as wholly physical and animal-like and grants that the slave has even the emotional and desiring part of the human soul, the properly analogous rule is that of intellect over appetites not soul over body. This rule is not despotic but is free like that of a king or a father,[23] and treats the subject not as a means but as an end in himself. This inconsistency may seem remote and technical because it depends on Aristotle's rather simplistic psychology, but it does provide further evidence of the difficulties Aristotle made for himself by trying to justify the treatment of some people as 'living tools'.

Aristotle's account of natural slavery is particularly vulnerable to criticism because his psychology makes the division between full human beings and slaves so sharp as to be incredible, even, at times, to Aristotle himself. If he has given one of the classic defences of genetic or racial supremacy, he has done it in a way that makes refutation easy; not all such doctrines are so readily refuted. To the modern reader who both abhors the institution of slavery and respects Aristotle's intellect, it may seem surprising, even morally reprehensible, that Aristotle does not accept the logical consequence of his difficulties and admit that slavery is unjustifiable. We must not forget, however, that he is writing within a society which took the existence of slavery for granted and where slaves, though they did not make up the entire labour force, were largely responsible for the marginal surplus of wealth and leisure which made Greek culture and civilization possible. Those thinkers who held that slavery was a matter of mere convention and was not based on any innate differences did not proceed to the obvious conclusion that slavery ought to be abolished. Indeed, no one, in the ancient world, as far as we know, advocated the abolition of slavery. Against the background of a general acceptance of slavery, the debate about whether

[22] I.5.vi (1254 b 4–6) 33.
[23] Cf. *EN* I.13 (1103 a 2–3).

slavery was natural was not, as it seems to us, about whether there should be slaves but about why there should be slaves. For Aristotle, slavery must be natural because the only justification for treating a man as less than a man is that he is actually in some way subhuman. The alternative view, that all men are equally men but some must accept being treated as less than men, he rejects as an immoral attempt to derive right from might. With this moral objection we would agree, though we would use it as an argument to prove that slavery is wrong and should not exist. But to Aristotle, with all his respect for the values of his own society, such a conclusion is unthinkable. Slavery must exist and must be justifiable; there must therefore be natural slaves. We can now understand why he tolerates a theory of slavery which is radically incoherent. He is convinced from the beginning that there are natural slaves. Any inconsistencies in his account of the natural slave would appear to him as minor difficulties still to be resolved by further work and revision; they would not be considered as in any way potentially destructive of the theory as a whole.

Women and Children

The head of the household also rules his wife and children. Whereas the rule over slaves is 'despotic' or in the master's own interests, rule over both wives and children is 'free' and is exercised in their interests not those of the head of the household. Women and children are not, however, treated in precisely the same way. Rule of the father over his children is similar to kingly rule because the father, though ruling in his children's interests, is naturally superior to them. Children have the deliberative faculty in their soul which makes them, unlike slaves, fully human and entitled to respect as people of independent value. But this faculty is 'undeveloped' or 'incomplete'[24] and so children are still dependent on their parents. Aristotle thus adopts the familiar and relatively uncontentious position that the immaturity of children requires them to be disciplined for their own good.

His attitude towards the role and status of women reflects, as we would expect, the attitudes prevalent in his own society. The proper area of women's activity is the house.[25] Greek women had no political and few legal rights and even within the house were under the general supervision of their husbands. Hence, male courage is shown in

---

[24] I.13.vii (1260 ^{a} 14) 52.
[25] II.5.xxiv (1264 ^{a} 40–b 6) 67; cf. *EN* V.6 (1134 ^{b} 15–18).

commanding, female courage in obeying.[26] Aristotle's one criticism of current attitudes to women is that the need to educate women in the values of the community has been neglected. Women constitute, after all, one-half of the free population.[27] The Spartans, who are commended for the public concern they show for education, are said to have suffered defeat partly because of their failure to educate their women.[28] The education of women, however, is not intended to take them out of their traditionally domestic and subservient role; it is to ensure that they perform this role effectively and in harmony with the general aims of the *polis*.

Aristotle's attempts to justify such a role for women are brief and unsatisfactory. Though he usually parades his differences with Plato, he gives very little attention to Plato's radical suggestion that women should be politically and socially equal except in so far as their physical difference from men is strictly relevant. Plato's justification of the equality of women is closely connected with, indeed is only made possible by, his abolition of the household. Aristotle, by supporting the retention of the household on the grounds of the value of personal family relationships and private property, is thereby committed to opposing the equality of women. He admits this openly.

To argue from an analogy with beasts and say that male and female ought to engage in the same occupations is futile: beasts do not have household duties.[29]

If the household is natural, so too must be the inferior status of women. As in the case of slaves and children, we would expect Aristotle to support such a belief by identifying the particular natural difference which makes women inferior to men. This he does only once and inadequately; whereas the slave has no deliberative faculty and the child has a deliberative faculty which is undeveloped, woman has a deliberative faculty which 'lacks authority'.[30] Aristotle gives us no reason why women's deliberative faculty should be without authority and completely ignores Plato's arguments about the intellectual equality of men and women. To the critical reader it seems that Aristotle is simply arguing from the fact of subjection to the existence of a natural inferiority which justifies subjection, an inference of right from might which he usually deplores.

[26] I.13.ix (1260 a 22–4) 52; cf. I.5.vii (1254 b 13–14) 33; III.4.xvii (1277 b 20–5) 110.
[27] I.13.xvi (1260 b 18–19) 54.   [28] II.9.v–xii (1269 b 12–1270 a 9) 84–5.
[29] II.5.xxiv (1264 b 4–6) 67.   [30] I.13.vii (1260 a 13) 52.

The same difficulty occurs with Aristotle's description of the rule of husband over wife as 'political' in contrast to the 'kingly' rule of father over children. Political rule involves a relationship of equality between ruler and ruled and therefore implies an alternation of ruling and being ruled. But in the case of husband and wife there is no such alternation; the husband always rules.[31] Aristotle tries to reconcile this permanent inequality with the equality implied by political rule by pointing out that whenever there is a relationship of ruler and ruled, even among equals, the ruler will always, by the very fact of his ruling, be distinct from and superior to the ruled. This distinction is usually accentuated by a difference of 'outward dignity, style of address and honour paid', and it is this difference which is said to exist between males and females. It is true that all forms of control by definition involve inequality, that when a leader is selected from a group of equals the previous equality has necessarily been destroyed and that the difference is commonly reinforced and increased by the symbols and trappings of authority. But if the inequality between husband and wife is due solely to the fact that one always rules while the other is always ruled, what prior justification is there for this permanent subjection of the one to the other? If there is no prior inequality, why should there not be, as in other types of political rule, an alternation of ruling and being ruled? Aristotle avoids this particular problem in the *Ethics* by comparing the role of husband over wife with aristocratic rather than political rule; aristocracy clearly implies superior virtue on the part of the ruler, though Aristotle admits that the husband will hand over to his wife responsibility for matters 'for which women are suited'.[32]

In some respects, Aristotle's treatment of the position of women is more culpable than his more commonly castigated justification of slavery. There, at least, the counter arguments are admitted and argued against, however unsuccessfully; here he is content with dogmatic assertion. In both cases we see how unshakeable is his belief in the value of the household and the family. Initially he derives the naturalness of the household from the supposed fact that the rule of husband over wife and of master over slave accord with innate characteristics in human beings. We can now see that he offers no convincing empirical evidence for the existence of these innate characteristics. Instead his belief in them seems to depend on the assumption that the household itself must be natural. Because the household meets what to Aristotle

[31] I.12.i–ii (1259 b 1–10) 49–50.
[32] *EN* VIII.10 (1160 b 32–5); 11 (1161 a 22–9).

are essential human needs, its relationships must be founded on natural differences, even if these are not readily discoverable by empirical observation.

Property and Wealth

Apart from the personal relationships of husband and wife, father and children, and master and slave, the other essential element of the household is the possession and acquisition of wealth. Though property is to be left in private hands, it is still the concern of political science and the statesman.[33] Like the moral behaviour of the members of the household, the economic activity of the household may affect the values and behaviour of the *polis* as a whole. Because the political community, in the sense of the institutions of government, has a responsibility for the over-all good of the *polis* it must ensure that the methods of using and acquiring wealth do not conflict with the public good. Private ownership of property does not entail complete economic freedom or *laissez faire*.

The principles which should govern the production of wealth are discussed in Book One[34] in terms of the relation of the art of acquisition (*chrematistike*) to household management (*oikonomike*). The question appears to be rather abstract, dealing with the relation of two branches of knowledge or skill, but it also has a more concrete application; it is another way of asking to what extent the head of the household (the practitioner of household management) should engage in acquiring material wealth (or make use of the art of acquisition). Aristotle considers three possibilities;[35] first, the art of acquisition may be identical with household management (i.e. the head of the household is solely concerned with acquisition); secondly, the art of acquisition may be part of household management (i.e. acquisition is one of the things with which the head of the household should be concerned); thirdly, the art of acquisition may be subordinate to household management (i.e. the head of the household, though concerned with the acquisition of wealth, uses it as a means towards other, more important purposes). Of these possibilities, Aristotle immediately rejects the first and supports the second[36] though he later seems to move towards the third. The head of the household will be concerned with acquiring wealth for his household but it will not be one of his major interests. He will be concerned more with the use of wealth than with its actual acquisition.[37] He

---

[33] Cf. II.5.v–viii (1263 ^{a} 21–38) 63. [34] I.8–11. [35] I.8.i (1256 ^{a} 3–5) 38.
[36] I.8.xiii–xv (1256 ^{b} 26–39) 40–1. [37] I.8.ii (1256 ^{a} 10–13) 38.

will oversee his own property but will leave most of the actual work to others in the same way as he will be generally concerned for the health of his family but will employ a doctor to minister to them.[38] This is the conclusion we should expect from Aristotle's conception of the good life which places no value on work in the sense of economic activity but does require, as a necessary condition, a certain level of material prosperity.

During his discussion of the art of acquisition, Aristotle distinguishes between acquisition which is justified and should properly be a concern of the head of the household and acquisition which should be avoided. This distinction is elaborated at some length and is the most important part of his theory of property. It depends, like so many of the arguments of Book One, on his view of nature. The natural world and all the natural species which it contains are organized according to a rational plan or order; 'nature does nothing without purpose.' All living things are provided by nature with the means of their own sustenance. Thus plants exist, at least in part, for the purpose of feeding animals and animals exist, at least in part, for the purpose of feeding and clothing human beings.[39] 'Natural' wealth is property which is naturally provided in this way for men and is confined to the products of land and sea, such as farm animals and their by-products, crops, fruits, and fish; it exists 'naturally' while unnatural wealth is 'gained by experience and skill.'[40] 'Unnatural' wealth is derived from exchange, from buying and selling and other commercial activities such as usury. In Aristotle's sketch of its development, exchange began as a method of acquiring necessary and natural goods, for example exchanging wine for corn.[41] This type of barter is justifiable because it is aimed at satisfying men's natural wants. But the expansion of trade led to the development of money which greatly facilitated the exchange of products; with the invention of money came the illegitimate and unnatural use of exchange which is aimed not at meeting essential needs but at acquiring the maximum financial profit.[42]

Aristotle's disapproval of this type of commercial exchange seems to rest partly on the objection that money is itself not intrinsically or naturally valuable but derives its value from mere convention; he quotes the story of Midas, who turned everything to gold, as an example of the

[38] I.10.iii (1258 a 31–4) 46.
[39] I.8.ix–xii (1256 b 10–22) 39–40.
[40] I.9.i (1257 a 3–5) 41.
[41] I.9.vi (1257 a 25–8) 42.
[42] I.9. ix (1257 a 41–b 5) 42–3.

folly of thinking that money is true wealth.[43] It is on these grounds that he singles out the usurer for special condemnation. Usury, the lending of money for interest, is the making of money from money itself. It is therefore even more unnatural than other forms of trade because it is a step further removed from nature. Retailers are at least using money to buy and sell objects of natural wealth but the usurer has lost even this contact with natural wealth.[44] But Aristotle's major objection is that commercial exchange is aimed at unlimited wealth. He assumes that there is a limit to the amount of agricultural wealth which can be stored. Once money becomes the measure of wealth, this constraint is removed because there is no limit to the amount of money that can be accumulated.[45] Traders are therefore induced to pursue unlimited wealth. Aristotle's objection to the unlimited pursuit of wealth is essentially moral. Though material prosperity is a necessary condition of the good life, a limited amount of wealth is quite sufficient. Any attempt to seek more than is necessary or to elevate the acquisition of wealth into an end in itself will confuse the necessities of life with the real purpose of life. In terms of Aristotle's familiar distinction it is to concentrate on 'life but not the good life'.[46] Aristotle also connects the pursuit of money with the pursuit of physical pleasure; excessive wealth is chiefly sought and used for gratifying bodily pleasure. The pursuit of money may corrupt the whole ethical character of men who pervert all virtues and skills by turning them into means of gaining wealth.[47] He is especially critical of small businessmen, of shopkeepers rather than merchants, of 'petty usurers' rather than bankers, and seems to consider that they are the people most corrupted by the desire for financial gain.

These arguments are of interest as an expression of the aristocratic attitude towards wealth, with its preference for landed property and its prejudice against trade and commerce; they have also been influential in the history of economic and social thought. But we need to ask whether they do more than express an attitude and whether they have any validity as arguments. The claim that agriculture is closer than commerce to nature carries conviction if we mean that it is concerned more directly with products and processes of natural growth which do not depend on human technology. Aristotle, it is true, underestimates the extent to which, even in his day, farming made use of technology. The grinding

[43] I.9.xi (1257 b 10–17) 43; cf. *EN* V.5 (1133 a 28–31).
[44] I.10.v (1258 b 2–8) 46.
[45] I.8.xiii–xiv (1256 b 26–34) 40; I.9.xiii (1257 b 23–7) 44.
[46] I.9.xvi (1257 b 41–1258 a 1) 44.
[47] I.9.xvi–xviii (1258 a 2–14) 44–5.

of corn, the making of wine, and the catching of fish all require some tools and techniques. None the less, though farming is not natural in the sense of being completely devoid of 'experience and skill', we may allow that it is more natural or closer to nature than the buying and selling of agricultural products. This does not prove that farming is superior to commerce. Aristotle, as we have seen, often assumes that what is natural is best but it does not follow, even from his own theory of nature, that what is natural in the sense of primitive or unaffected by human technology is therefore best for man. When arguing that the *polis* or the relationships of the household are natural, he tries to show that they are in accordance with certain innate needs and capacities but he does not deny a role to human contrivance. He approves of civilization as the Greeks understood it and does not advocate any 'return to nature' in the sense of a rejection of civilized life. Yet the logical implication of the argument about natural property would be a complete rejection of civilization and a return to the primitive. We must assume that the desire to prove that agricultural wealth is morally superior has led him to adopt a view of nature which he would normally disown.

The other main argument is that agricultural wealth is limited whereas the profits of commerce are unlimited. Though we may grant that it is much easier to go on accumulating wealth in money than in produce, it is quite possible to continue increasing holdings of land and it is not impossible to hoard unlimited amounts of some types of agricultural produce, such as corn. Aristotle is also wrong in equating the products of farming with basic human necessities as if farmers were never concerned with the production of luxuries. If he believes on ethical grounds that it is wrong to pursue more than a certain level of material prosperity, then he would have done better to argue for a limit to the general acquisition of wealth instead of trying to maintain that one type of acquisition is intrinsically limited. Similarly, if money is not the only type of wealth which may be accumulated in greater quantity than is necessary or proper, there is no justification for singling out the trader as the man who pursues unlimited profit. Indeed, even if this were the only pursuit in which unlimited profit were possible, this would not prove that he actually does aim at unlimited wealth. Thus Aristotle's attempt to prove that traders are more concerned with profit and material gain than farmers is unsuccessful. This does not mean, however, that his conclusion is false. The view that farming, especially when relatively primitive in technology, is less oriented than retailing and commerce towards profit is one that has been widely held in different historical periods, not just by aristocrats but, more recently, by radical critics of modern capitalism. But though it may contain an element of truth, it needs to be tested by sociological investigation not proved by *a priori* argument.

Aristotle's arguments against retailing and commerce seem to imply that such activities are to be completely banished from the *polis*. Yet the level of civilization necessary for the good life could hardly be provided without some reliance on traders. Indeed, in Book Seven, when describing the ideal *polis*, Aristotle admits that there will be trading, both internally within the city and externally with other states. He does not try to exclude traders altogether but confines himself to limiting their influence within the state.[48] In Book One, however, he is not asking whether trading is necessary for the *polis* as a whole but whether the head of the household will engage in trade. He is concerned with the personal conduct of the head of the household who, ideally, will be someone who has achieved human happiness and is living the good life. The conclusion that such people should possess agricultural wealth and not engage in trade does not necessarily imply that no trading should be conducted at all. In the ideal state there are many functions which are necessary but which, because they are in some way not worthy of the character and abilities of the good man, should be performed by people who are not full members of the state and do not share fully in the purposes for which the city exists. It is therefore beside the point to criticize Aristotle for ignoring or misinterpreting the social function of trade in Book One. He is not concerned with the social usefulness of trade, which he elsewhere acknowledges, but with its effect on the individual, which he deplores. This focus on ethical effect rather than social function explains why Aristotle is particularly contemptuous of the small-scale businessman, in modern terms the *petit bourgeois*. Such a person, though engaged in the same economic activity as the wealthy businessman, the *haut bourgeois*, has to spend more of his time directly involved with his business and his character is therefore likely to be more infected by business values.

It is significant that the longest section in the *Politics* which Aristotle devotes to what we would call 'economics' is primarily ethical in approach. He seems to be very aware of the influence of economic factors on human behaviour, both on the personal and on the political level; he considers that the major political conflict in the states of his

[48] VII.6.iv–v (1327 a 25–40) 268; VII.12.iii–vi (1331 a 30–b 4) 280–1; cf. VI.8.iii (1321 b 14–18) 250.

time is between the rich and the poor and that the regulation of production and wealth is one of the major functions of the statesman. But though he is aware of economic factors, he does not see them as such. He does not think, as we do, of the 'economy' as something separate and independent which may affect or be affected by politics. Indeed, he does not have the concept of an 'economy', of a pattern or structure of behaviour concerned solely with production and wealth and operating, at least in the abstract, according to its own independent rules. This is a modern concept which was unknown to the Greeks and to Aristotle. For Aristotle, 'economics' (*oikonomike*) still carries its original meaning of household management and is not exclusively concerned with economic questions. Wealth and production are aspects of the general life of the *polis* like education, warfare, or drama and so are equally subject to ethical evaluation and political control. The question of 'economics' in Aristotle illustrates a more general difficulty which we face when we try to understand Greek political thought. We tend to divide our thoughts and activities into different, autonomous categories such as the economic, the religious, the moral, the legal, the political, and the educational. For the Greeks some of these distinctions did not exist and those that did were much more blurred than they are for us. Greek society, we may say, was more 'integrated', less 'differentiated', than our own. Though we cannot avoid using words like 'economics' when we discuss Aristotle's political theory we must not let them distort his meaning. At the same time, the absence of such sharp distinctions in his view of society may help us to a better understanding of our own society. Though more differentiated than Greek society, it is not so sharply divided as our categories sometimes suggest. Aristotle's approach to politics reminds us that the spheres of economics, law, morality, and education are not isolated but closely interdependent.

CHAPTER FOUR
CONSTITUTIONS

In Book Three, when Aristotle turns to questions about actual government and politics, he makes what appears to be a completely fresh start and gives a new account of the parts and definition of the *polis* in terms of the citizen (*polites*) and the constitution (*politeia*). Book Three was probably written quite independently of Book One, but this does not mean that the two books contradict each other to any significant extent. There is an essential continuity of ideas between them and the differing accounts of the parts of the *polis* are to be regarded as complementary rather than alternative. The change in approach is due simply to a change in the type of question being asked. As the focus narrows and the questions become more specific, further concepts and distinctions become necessary. In Book One Aristotle was primarily interested in the general nature of the *polis* and its relation to other communities, especially the household. In Book Three he is more concerned with government and political institutions.

Citizenship

When the Greeks referred, for example, to the state of Athens, they said 'the Athenians' not 'Athens'. As a political entity, the Greek *polis* consisted of its citizens and Aristotle therefore begins his new account of the *polis* with the question, 'What is a citizen?'[1] He starts his search for the definition of citizenship by eliminating certain mistaken conceptions.[2] Simple residence in a particular place does not make a man a citizen because this characteristic is shared by non-citizens such as slaves and resident aliens. Nor does possession of the legal rights arising out of commercial contracts, such as the rights of suing and being sued, make someone a citizen. Such rights may be enjoyed 'under the provision of a treaty', that is by aliens who are not citizens of the particular state. The rights which are characteristic of citizenship, he suggests, are certain political rights, the right to share in the administration of justice and the right to share in political office (*arche*).[3]

But what sort of political office? The Greek word *arche* is wide in

[1] III.1–3.
[2] III.1.iii–v (1275 a 7–19) 102.
[3] III.1.vi (1275 a 22–3) 102.

meaning and can mean simply 'rule' in a general sense, as in the different types of 'rule', or, more specifically, 'office' or 'magistracy'. Some people, says Aristotle, may be unwilling to call members of an assembly or of a popular court 'office-holders' or 'magistrates', but it would be absurd to deny that members of these powerful bodies 'rule'.[4] To help identify the type of political office which provides a qualification for citizenship, he distinguishes between definite or specified and indefinite or unspecified office. Definite offices can be held only for a fixed period of time whereas tenure of indefinite office, such as membership of a deliberative assembly or a popular court, is for an indefinite period. He then defines citizenship in terms of possession of indefinite office.[5] But this definition too is only interim; he immediately points out that it is of limited application. It may provide a satisfactory definition of a citizen in a democracy but not in other constitutions where there may be no regular meetings of the popular assembly or where lawsuits may be decided by different groups of magistrates. In states such as Sparta or Carthage the powers of deliberation and adjudication are exercised by holders of definite rather than indefinite office and it is these powers which seem to be especially connected with citizenship. Aristotle therefore amends his definition to 'those who are entitled to take part in deliberative or judicial office'.[6] Thus the essential characteristic of a citizen is not membership of indefinite office but participation, or more precisely the right of participation, in the political functions of deliberation and adjudication. This definition is still most suited to more popular forms of government. In kingships or oligarchies, for example, deliberative and judicial powers may be restricted to a very small group and there may be people outside this group, particularly members of the militia, who would still be counted as citizens.

Though the definition of citizenship is not completely accurate, it does have the advantage of being purely descriptive and value-free. Using the example of the new citizens created in Athens by Cleisthenes from among the ranks of foreigners and slaves, Aristotle clearly distinguishes the question of who is a citizen from the question of who ought to be a citizen. He admits that there may be uncertainty whether those who ought not to be citizens really are citizens on the grounds that 'wrong and false mean the same thing.'[7] But under his definition there can be no doubt that those who share in deliberative or judicial office are citizens, whether justly or unjustly. Aristotle is thus rejecting

---

[4] III.1.vii (1275 a 26–9) 102–3.   [5] III.1.viii (1275 a 32–3) 103.
[6] III.1.xii (1275 b 18–20) 103–4.   [7] III.2.iv (1276 a 1–2) 104.

his usual method of defining a species in terms of its best or ideal instance. This approach was useful, for example in the general theory of the *polis,* when he was trying to elaborate political values and ideals, but it is less satisfactory when he intends to describe and analyse political phenomena both good and bad. The same concern for a less evaluative terminology is shown in his definition of the *polis* at the beginning of Book Three in terms of a group of citizens self-sufficient for the purpose of life.[8] This definition differs from that given in Book One where the *polis* is self-sufficient not only for the purposes of life but also for those of the good life. The earlier account of the proper purpose of the *polis* has not been forgotten[9] but, by restricting the purpose of the *polis* to the provision of the necessities of life, Aristotle provides a wider definition which will clearly cover all existing states, regardless of their quality or value.

The Constitution

The account of citizenship and the *polis* leads directly to a discussion of the constitution. Aristotle raises the problem of what makes a group of people a *polis* and concludes that the constitution is the only factor which will adequately account for the identity of the *polis.* He reaches this conclusion by the familiar method of eliminating unsatisfactory possibilities. It would be a mistake to say that the *polis* is to be identified in terms of its territory. The inhabitants of the same *polis* may change their locality or may be split into different territories.[10] Moreover, even when a body of men do inhabit the same territory the mere fact that they are surrounded by a wall does not make them into a *polis*; it would be possible to surround the whole of the Peloponnese (the southern peninsula of Greece which contained a large number of separate states) with a wall but this would not make it into a single *polis.*[11] The clue is to be found in the fact that the *polis* is a *koinonia* whose members are citizens. Citizens share in the political functions of citizenship and these functions are determined by the constitution (*politeia*). Hence it is the constitution which determines the identity of the *polis* and when the constitution has changed the *polis* has also changed.

For, since the *polis* is a community of citizens in a constitution, when the constitution of the citizens changes and becomes different in kind, the *polis* also does. We may compare this with a chorus, which may at

[8] III.1.xii (1275 ^{b} 20–1) 104.
[9] III.6.iii–v (1278 ^{b} 17–30) 114; III.9.xiii–xiv (1280 ^{b} 39–1281 ^{a} 4) 121.
[10] III.3.iii (1276 ^{a} 19–22) 105.   [11] III.3.v (1276 ^{a} 24–30) 105.

one time perform in a tragedy and at another in a comedy and so be different in kind, yet all the while be composed of the same persons.[12]

The political community, as we have seen, like all communities involves joint activity for a common purpose but is distinguished from other communities by the fact that it has supreme authority. Similarly, the notion of a 'constitution', which defines a political community, also involves both a common purpose and a supreme authority. Aristotle's fullest definition of 'constitution' is

the arrangement which states adopt for the distribution of offices of power and for the determination of the sovereign and of the end at which the community aims.[13]

The two aspects of the constitution are clearly identified: the ethical, concerned with the aim pursued by the community, and the institutional, including the structure of political institutions and the distribution of power. In combining these different elements within the concept of a constitution, Aristotle is following Greek usage. The Greeks had no clear distinction, as we have, between the legal and the ethical—a further example of the comparative lack of differentiation in Greek society. When Greeks thought, for example, of the Spartan 'constitution', they thought not only of the powers of the kings and the council and other institutional arrangements but also of the Spartan way of life and the ideals it expressed. As Aristotle says, the constitution of a city is 'the way it lives.'[14] Today most would consider the constitution to be a purely institutional concept. Yet, even now, if we wish to understand the politics of a country, we must look beyond the constitutional framework to the motives of those who use it and ultimately to the aims and values of the community as a whole. If we want to estimate the merits of a particular constitution we cannot study it in isolation from its social context. This is a lesson which modern political science, dominated for so long by a narrowly legalistic approach, has found difficult to learn. Modern social life, though less integrated than the life of the Greek *polis,* is not so divided that the studies of constitutional law and sociology can be treated as wholly autonomous and unrelated. By using 'constitution' in this wider sense, Aristotle reminds us of the inseparable connection between institutions and social values.

The concept of 'constitution', though it has ethical connotations, is still a descriptive concept, referring to the actual values of particular

[12]   III.3.vii (1276 ^{b} 1–6) 106.
[13]   IV.1.x (1289 ^{a} 15–18) 151.   [14]   IV.11.iii (1295 ^{a} 40–^{b} 1) 171.

communities without implying preference for any particular set of values. The aims and values of a particular constitution are not valuable absolutely but only to the members of that constitution. We have seen how Aristotle deliberately gives a definition of citizenship which is not value-laden and does not force one to say that those who ought not to be citizens are not really citizens; citizenship is determined by the rules of the community. Similarly, constitutions themselves can be of different varieties, bad as well as good.[15] This is the main implication of the long discussion about whether the virtue of the good man is the same as that of the good citizen.[16] Within any *polis,* the citizens ought to be united in pursuit of the common good of the community and the virtue of the good citizen will consist in helping to pursue this good and preserve his constitution. The virtue of the citizen is therefore relative to the virtue of the constitution of which he is a member and may, if the constitution is a bad one, involve the pursuit of undesirable aims. The good man, on the other hand, is absolutely, not relatively, virtuous and his virtue can be the same as that of the good citizen only in a constitution which is itself good. To us the interest of this distinction may lie in the implication of a clash between moral principle and the citizen's duty to the state and in the consequent problem of political obedience. But Aristotle is not interested in this problem and is simply concerned to point out that different constitutions enshrine different values and that the values of a particular constitution are not necessarily good.

The institutional, as distinct from the ethical, aspect of the constitution is covered in the first part of Aristotle's definition: the arrangement for the distribution of offices and for the determination of the sovereign. The most important institution determined by the constitution is the body that is supreme or sovereign (*kurion*). This body is sometimes described as the 'civic body' (*politeuma*), which exercises such an influence on the whole of the constitution that it may be identified with the constitution.[17] The supremacy of the civic body needs to be understood within Aristotle's general view of the institutional structure. Though he sometimes talks as if the civic body were the sole ruling or decision-making body in the *polis,* this is an over-simplification. In Book Four he describes three parts or elements which every constitution must contain: the deliberative, the official or magisterial and the judicial.[18] Of these, the first and last, the deliberative and judicial,

---

[15] III.1.ix (1275 a 38–b 3) 103.   [16] III.4.
[17] III.6.i (1278 b 11) 113; cf. III.7.ii (1279 a 25–7) 115.   [18] IV.14–16.

which involve the powers especially associated with citizenship, are supreme.[19] The most important part is the deliberative which has four functions:[20] first, it is responsible for the most important decisions in foreign policy, matters of war and peace and the making and breaking of alliances; secondly, it has certain legal functions concerned with the making and interpretation of laws; thirdly, it administers the more severe penalties such as death, exile, and confiscation of property; fourthly, it deals with the election of magistrates and their examination after they have completed their turn of office. The powers associated with deliberation are thus wide and comprehensive and it is easy to see why Aristotle should sometimes regard this branch of government alone as supreme.[21] It may not be concerned with every single political decision but it retains control over all major areas of government. In particular, it limits the initiative and autonomy of the other two elements, the magistrates and the courts, by controlling the laws which regulate their functions and by retaining the power to decide the most important 'executive' and 'judicial' questions.

Aristotle's classification of the elements of government, particularly his account of the deliberative element, must be carefully distinguished from a number of apparently similar doctrines in modern constitutional theory. First, his threefold division is not the same as the modern division of the functions of government into three parts, legislative, executive, and judicial. The deliberative element, as we have seen, involves all three functions, executive and judicial as well as legislative. Moreover, though the deliberative element may have the power of legislation,[22] this is not its most important power. Aristotle does not see legislation as an especially significant part of the day-to-day workings of government and would not agree with the constitutional theory that considers legislation to be the main method of declaring public policy. Though legislation has become much more frequent and is a more vital part of the daily operations of government than it was in Aristotle's time, the emphasis he gives to other types of decision making, such as appointing officials or deciding matters of war and peace, is still relevant for political scientists. 'Legislative supremacy' is to a certain extent a modern myth, a product of such struggles as that of the British Parliament with the Crown, and the attempt to regard the making of laws as

[19] e.g. III.11.xv (1282 a 23–9) 126; cf. *Rhetoric* I.8 (1365 b 26–8).
[20] IV.14.iii (1298 a 3–7) 179.
[21] e.g. IV.14.xvi (1299 a 1) 182; cf. II.6.ii (1264 b 33–4) 68.
[22] IV.14.v (1298 a 21) 179.

the main method of political control for a long time hampered the realistic analysis of decision-making in the modern state. Aristotle would also not accept the sharp distinction, implied by the modern notion of 'executive', between the making and the execution of political decisions or between 'policy' and 'administration'. The view that the executive must limit itself to carrying out the will of the legislator may be a potent and beneficial myth but it cannot be an accurate description of the political facts. Aristotle does not view the relation of the various individual magistracies to the deliberative element in this simplistic way and the translation 'executive' for the second, official or magisterial, element of government is therefore misleading. The deliberative exercises control over officials by means of procedures such as election and scrutiny but Aristotle does not pretend that officials do no more than implement the will of the deliberative body. They are themselves involved in deliberation and adjudication as well as in their more characteristic function of 'ordering'.[23]

Secondly, though Aristotle's phrase for the supreme body, *to kurion,* is commonly translated as 'the sovereign', such a translation will mislead if it suggests certain doctrines associated with modern theories of sovereignty. Politically, the term 'sovereign' implies that there is one and only one person or group of persons in a community who exercise political power. As we have seen the supremacy of the civic body is relative rather than absolute. It decides the most important political issues and has a measure of indirect control over the decisions made by the holders of other offices. But Aristotle does not try to suggest that it is the sole source of political power and control. As a term in legal theory, 'sovereign' implies a person or body that is the source of all law and therefore by definition not subject to legal limits; being the creator of law it is above the law. Aristotle does not see the relation between the supreme body and the laws in this way. He distinguishes between states where the supreme body governs in accordance with law and those where it does not. In the former case, the supreme body acts within the already established legal code and can hardly be said to be legally sovereign. The characteristic of legal sovereignty therefore cannot be attributed to all supreme bodies. Moreover, to describe even those governments that are unrestricted by law as legally sovereign may not be very illuminating. The modern concept of legal sovereignty and its opposite, the concept of constitutionally limited government, depend

[23] IV.15.iv (1299 ª 25–8) 183.

on the technical question of legal validity, on whether or not any
measure passed by the legislature can be declared legally invalid. Aristotle
is more concerned with the general manner in which the government
conducts its business. He sees governments whose actions are not subject
to legal limits not just as legally unrestricted but as essentially lawless.
Except in the unusual case of the absolute king, they are extreme forms
of perverted constitutions in which the ruler or rulers govern according
to their own whims by means of *ad hoc* and unpredictable decrees.
Government under the law, on the other hand, is orderly and just. In
spite of his emphasis on the legislator and the rule of law, Aristotle's
approach to political analysis is not a legalistic one. Though this may
sometimes make his theory seem imprecise, yet it also saves him from
some of the unrealistic and confusing fictions by which political analysis
has often been distorted.

Classification of Constitutions

The definition of a constitution provides the basis for a division of
constitutions into different types. Because of his general interest in
problems of classification, Aristotle discusses the classification of
constitutions at some length and makes a major contribution to this
aspect of political science. His initial classification of constitutions is a
sixfold one, formed by appling two criteria: first, the size of the civic
body, one, few, or many, and secondly, whether the rulers rule with a
view to the common interest or to their own interest. The resulting six
types are: the rule of one in the common interest (kingship); the rule of
the few in the common interest (aristocracy); the rule of the many in
the common interest (polity); the rule of one in his own interest
(tyranny); the rule of the few in their own interest (oligarchy); the rule
of the many in their own interest (democracy).[24] Though Aristotle
later modifies this classification, it is never competely superseded. It is
based on contemporary usage and fits closely with his own definition of
a constitution. The first criterion concerns the institutional aspect of
the constitution, the size of the supreme body; the second concerns the
end or purpose of the constitution. Neither criterion, however, is
unambiguous in meaning. First, there is a difficulty in the precise
meaning of the few and the many. They are relative terms, meaning
minority and majority or the lesser and the greater part, but Aristotle
does not explicitly define the group from which the greater or lesser

[24] III.7.iii–v (1279 a 32–b 10) 115–16.

part may the taken. He certainly does not mean to include those people whose life is confined to the household, namely women, children, and slaves. It is also unlikely that he would include resident aliens or foreigners who were usually considered to be political outsiders and therefore not potential candidates for citizenship. The group which he probably has in mind consists of those free adult males who are not aliens and who in most Greek states would be considered citizens. But under his definition of citizenship this group cannot be identified with the citizen body. Because he defines citizenship in terms of participation in deliberative and judicial office, the citizen body in any constitution will be coextensive with the supreme body. Thus, for example, when the few rule they cannot strictly speaking be a few of the citizens because only they, the members of the supreme body, will be citizens. This difficulty is an unnoticed consequence of Aristotle's slightly unusual definition of citizenship but it does not seriously affect the clarity of his classification.

Secondly, what does Aristotle mean by rule 'in the common interest'? He equates the common interest with absolute justice,[25] by which he probably means justice in the wider or 'universal' sense, that is complete social virtue. The common interest is therefore another description of the true purpose of the *polis*. He also refers to the common interest as if it were the interest of all the citizens as distinct from the interest of the rulers only[26] which again raises the problem of who the citizens are. On Aristotle's definition of citizenship, the citizens are those who are members of the citizen body and will usually be the ruling body. Does he really mean to imply that a narrow oligarchy which restricts all citizenship rights to its own members will therefore be ruling in the common interest? Considering his identification of the common interest with absolute justice this is most unlikely and we must assume the common interest to be in the interests not of all who happen to be citizens but rather of all who ought to be citizens and whose interests ought to be considered.

As the difference between rule in the common interest and rule in the rulers' interests depends on Aristotle's theory of the true and natural purpose of the *polis*, he describes the two types as 'normal' or 'correct' and 'perverted' rule. At the same time, he recalls his earlier discussion of the different types of rule; he associates 'normal' government with

[25] III.6.xi (1279 a 17–19) 115; cf. III.12.i (1282 b 16–18) 128; III.13.iii (1283 a 37–40) 130.

[26] III.7.ii (1279 a 31–2) 115; III.13.xii (1283 b 40–2) 131.

rule over free men because it is in the interests of the ruled as well as the rulers while 'perverted' governments are despotic because they are wholly concerned with the interests of the rulers.[27] Thus, though he has been careful to choose definitions of citizenship and the constitution which will cover bad as well as good instances, his earlier theory of the moral purpose of the *polis* has not been forgotten but plays a central role in the classification of constitutions. We should remember that for Aristotle the use of an evaluative criterion such as this does not imply any loss of objectivity. Whether a civic body rules in the common interest or not is for him as much a matter of fact as the numerical size of the civic body.

The initial version of the sixfold classification is neat and symmetrical. But it does not satisfy Aristotle because it does not catch the true essence of the different constitutional types. While naming the six main types, he supplements the bare mathematical notion of the size of the supreme group with a description of the group's main social characteristics.[28] Understandably, this does not apply to the monarchical types, kingship and tyranny, where an individual rather than a group is sovereign. But in each of the other four the ruling group has a certain character. In aristocracy (literally 'rule of the best men'), the rulers, as the name suggests, are men of virtue who will be able to provide a virtuous type of government directed to the common good. In oligarchy the ruling group will be the rich, in democracy the poor, both ruling in their own interests. What group dominates in a polity, the good form of rule of the many? If it is a good constitution, then the rulers must be good men. But Aristotle thinks there cannot be more than a few really virtuous people in any community. The only type of virtue which can be spread over a wide area in the community is military virtue which belongs to those who possess arms, the 'hoplites' or heavy infantry who are drawn from citizens of moderate wealth. Aristotle thus reveals his conviction that the rule of the majority cannot be good unless a majority are wealthy enough to possess hoplite arms and he prepares the way for his later identification of the polity with the constitution of the middle class and as a mixture of oligarchy and democracy.

The description of oligarchy and democracy as rule by the rich and the poor respectively immediately raises a difficulty. If democracy is said to be the rule of the poor as well as the rule of the many, what are we to call a constitution where the many who are ruling are wealthy

[27] III.6.v–xi (1278 b 30–1279 a 21) 114–15.
[28] III.7.iii–v (1279 a 32–b 10) 115–16.

rather than poor? The same problem may arise with oligarchy. How are we to describe a constitution where the rulers are few but poor rather than wealthy? The two criteria, numerical size and relative amount of property, cannot both mark the difference between oligarchy and democracy because, if they did, there could be constitutions which were neither democracies nor oligarchies. Aristotle's first answer in Book Three is that wealth and poverty are the essential determinants of oligarchy and democracy while the size of the civic body is an accidental characteristic which can vary without affecting the nature of the constitution.[29] Because the wealthy are usually few and the poor usually many, the real difference between the two types of constitutions has been obscured and an accidental characteristic has become an essential one.

Aristotle also adds a dominant principle for each type of constitution. This principle has two aspects. It involves both the general end or goal pursued by the community and also the principle or criterion according to which power and other goods are distributed in the community. Thus, in the case of oligarchy, the dominant principle is wealth. Wealth is what the rulers pursue; it is the state's aim.[30] Wealth is also the distributive principle for honour and political power; all political offices typically involve a high property qualification.[31] Similarly with aristocracy, virtue is both the goal of the state and the qualification for office.[32] The dominant principle in democracy is freedom. As a goal, democratic freedom is the freedom to do as one likes.[33] As a distributive principle, freedom involves free birth,[34] the status of a free man in a community where slavery is practised; in a democracy citizenship and office ought to be open to all men of free birth.

With both oligarchy and aristocracy there is a close parallel between the dominant principle and the social characteristics of the dominant group: wealth and the wealthy, virtue and the virtuous. In the case of democracy, symmetry would demand that the dominant principle be poverty. But symmetry would mislead. The democrats do not claim poverty as a principle in the same way that oligarchs claim wealth and aristocrats virtue. Conversely, it would be wrong to equate the group with the principle and to describe democracy as the rule of the free born. Rather it is the majority of the free born who rule in a democracy

[29] III.8.vii−viii (1280 a 1−4) 117.   [30] Cf. V.10.xi (1311 a 9−10) 218.
[31] III.8.vii−viii (1280 a 1−6) 117.
[32] III.17.iv (1288 a 9−12) 146; III.18.i (1288 a 32−41) 147.
[33] V.9.xv (1310 a 30−4) 216; VI.2.iii (1317 b 11−13) 237.
[34] III.8.vii−viii (1280 a 1−6) 117.

and this majority are usually to be identified with the poor who rule in their own interest. Aristotle believes that political conflicts of his day are principally due to a clash between two economic groups, the rich and the poor who support two different types of constitution (oligarchy and democracy) with different political principles (wealth and freedom). His scheme of classification must fit this conviction even if it thereby loses some logical symmetry.

Aristotle pays less attention to the principles of the remaining types of constitution. He does not explicitly give a distributive principle for either of the monarchical types but he does briefly mention an aim for each. The king aims at honour while the tyrant aims at pleasure.[35] Polity is not given a clearly distinct principle. If it is counted as a mixed constitution, partly oligarchy and partly democracy, then we can assume that its principles are themselves a mixture. Certainly, its distributive principles involve a balanced compromise between wealth and free birth and presumably its aim will be a certain amount of wealth combined with a certain amount of personal freedom.

The sixfold classification is too general to accommodate the variety of existing constitutions. To supplement it, Aristotle describes sub-types of each general type, for example five types of kingship, four each of oligarchy and democracy and so on. But there are still not enough categories to enable every actual constitution to be clearly classified as an instance of a particular species or type. To meet this difficulty, Aristotle's categories become increasingly formal and abstract. The development may be illustrated by his approach to the unusual case where power is in the hands of a rich majority or a poor minority. His solution to this problem in Book Three, as we have seen, is that the economic criterion is essential; where the rich rule, whether they are few or many, there is oligarchy; where the poor rule, whether many or few, there is democracy; number is merely an accidental characteristic. The wealthy are usually, but need not be, few; the poor are usually, but need not be, many. But when the same question is raised again in Book Four, Aristotle answers it differently by saying that both criteria are essential; oligarchy implies the rule of both the few and the wealthy and democracy entails the rule of both a majority and the poor.[36] The later passage has been criticized on the grounds that, by making both criteria essential, it fails to cater for the unusual case where the rich are many and the poor few. This problem, it is held,

[35] V.10.ix (1311 ^{a} 4–5) 218.
[36] IV.4.vi (1290 ^{b} 17–20) 155.

cannot be solved unless only one criterion is made essential as in Book Three.

The earlier solution, however, by solving one problem raises another, just as difficult, at least in connection with democracy. If democracy is simply rule of the poor and has no essential connection with the rule of the majority, can the dominant democratic principle still be freedom? If, in accordance with the democratic principle of freedom, office and power are to be distributed equally to all of free birth, then democracies will necessarily involve majority rule. Therefore, if freedom is essential to democracy, there seems to be an essential connection between democracy and the many. The same point does not arise directly with oligarchy because its principle, wealth, does not logically imply a minority in the same way as freedom, the democratic principle, logically implies a majority. But we might think, and surely Aristotle would also have thought, that there is something rather paradoxical about saying that 'oligarchy', literally 'rule by a few', has no essential connection with the notion of minority rule.

The earlier solution, that only the economic criterion is essential, is thus not free from difficulties. Consequently, the later solution, that both criteria are essential, is not so obviously unsatisfactory. Indeed it is not unsatisfactory at all if we do not expect every possible individual constitution to fit neatly into a particular category or type. This expectation Aristotle has now given up. He now assumes that there are a number of different characteristics essential to a given constitutional type and concedes that a given instance may possess characteristics belonging to more than one general type. The constitution where a rich majority or a poor minority rule will be in one respect an oligarchy and in another a democracy. There is no longer any need to say that it belongs categorically to one type or the other. By making this change Aristotle has given up looking for a classification like the biologist's which will describe all existing species and where each living thing will fit clearly and unequivocally into one category. Instead, his categories have become abstract models, like the ideal types of modern social theory such as 'the market economy' or 'the tribal society'. Though based on observation, they are not descriptions of any actual institutions.

A similar development can be seen in Aristotle's description of constitutional sub-types. The first general type to be subdivided is kingship.[37] Though some of the types are described as partly kingly and partly

[37] III.14.

tyrannical, which implies that 'kingship' and 'tyranny' are being used as abstract models, most of the five types of kingship are meant to be descriptions of actually existing constitutions. Kingship, however, is a form of government relatively rare and remote from Aristotle's interests. In later books, when he turns to the commonest Greek constitutions, oligarchy and democracy, the classification of sub-types is quite different. One of the sub-types of democracy is described as extreme democracy and is an abstract representation of all the democratic characteristics in their extreme or pure form. At the other end of the scale is a moderate democracy with oligarchic features and bordering on the 'polity' which is a balanced mixture of oligarchy and democracy. The other two types of democracy lie in between these two poles. The types of oligarchy similarly range from the moderate to the extreme. Paradoxically, as Aristotle becomes more interested in actual constitutions and the amount of evidence increases, his classification becomes more abstract and less empirical.

The account of the three elements of government, to which we have already referred, also implies a more flexible approach to classification. The initial classification of constitutions depended on the assumption that there was one supreme group or person. But when, in Book Four, Aristotle analyses the deliberative, official and judicial elements, he gives a much more complex picture of the structure of government. For instance, the four main functions of the deliberative element dealing respectively with foreign policy, law, adjudication, and officials, may be performed by the same body or official or may be shared between several. Qualifications for these bodies or offices may differ and so too may the method of appointment. The official and judicial elements encompass a similar variety of spheres of competence, qualifications, and methods of appointment. Each difference in any one of these elements leads to a difference in the constitution but Aristotle does not try to list and classify all the possible permutations and combinations. Instead, he classifies certain institutional arrangements as typical of certain general types of constitution, such as oligarchy and democracy, and allows that individual constitutions may incorporate features from more than one type. In this way he is able to use his classification to describe a wide variety of actual constitutions without making the number of categories unmanageably large and so negating the organizing and simplifying purpose of classification.

How useful Aristotle's categories are for analysing particular constitutions may be illustrated by an extract from his description of the Carthaginian constitution.

Then there are *oligarchic* features: the committee of five, the Pentarchies, which have control over many important matters, not only fill up vacancies on their own by co-option but appoint members of the Hundred, the highest constitutional authority. Moreover they enjoy a longer tenure of office than the rest; they begin to exercise authority before they become members of the committee and continue to do so after they have ceased to be members. On the other hand we must allow as *aristocratic* the fact that they receive no pay and are not chosen by lot, and one or two other features of that kind; for example all lawsuits are decided by these committees, not, as at Sparta, some by one set of persons, others by another. The most conspicuous divergence of the Carthaginian constitution from the *aristocratic* towards the *oligarchic* is one which is quite in accord with the mentality of the Carthaginians in general; they believe that rulers should be chosen not merely from the best people but also from the wealthiest. It is impossible, they argue, for a man without ample means either to be a good ruler or to have the leisure to be one. Now if it is accepted that election according to wealth is *oligarchic,* according to merit *aristocratic,* this then must be a third principle and one which is constitutionally imposed on the Carthaginians. For they have both these in mind, merit and wealth, when they elect, particularly when they elect the highest officers, kings and generals.[38]

We can see how the general types, in this case the types of oligarchy and aristocracy, are used to illuminate the unique instance. The Carthaginian constitution does not completely fit any of the major constitutional categories. Yet by showing how far and in what ways it approximates to different types, Aristotle is able to use a simple classification to reveal the major characteristics of a complex constitution.

Kingship and Tyranny

The characteristics of each of the six main categories of constitution and of their respective sub-types or species may now be briefly described. Kingship and tyranny may conveniently be taken together because Aristotle sometimes does so himself and because the nature of each is largely revealed by its contrast with the other. Both are species of 'monarchy', the rule of one man, but they differ in the type of interest pursued by the ruler. Kings govern in the common interest while tyrants govern in their own interest.[39] The rule of the tyrant is thus despotic, like the rule of the master over his slave, whereas the rule of the king is a type of 'free' rule, like that of a father over his children.

---

[38] II.11.vii–ix (1273 ^{a} 13–30) 95–6.
[39] III.7.iii; v (1279 ^{a} 32–3; ^{b} 6–7) 116; V.10.ix (1311 ^{a} 2–4) 218.

Kings rule over willing subjects but tyrants over unwilling subjects;[40] the king pursues honour, the tyrant pleasure.[41] Wealth is also important to the tyrant because it is needed both for his own luxurious self-indulgence and for his own security. Being unable to rely on the support of his fellow citizens, he is forced to employ mercenaries as a body-guard.[42] The insecurity felt by tyrants means that self-protection becomes of great importance; indeed Aristotle once, in the *Rhetoric*, describes it as the end of tyranny[43] though usually be considers it a means rather than an end.

Aristotle distinguishes five types of kingship.[44] The first is kingship on the Spartan pattern where the kings are responsible for military and religious matters only. But because it could exist within any general type of constitution, it is, in Aristotle's opinion, more a type of general-ship than a type of kingship.[45] The second is a type common among barbarians and is a mixture of kingship and tyranny. It is tyrannical because the nature of the rule is despotic and the people are servile in character. The rulers, however, are accepted by their subjects and are able to employ citizens for their bodyguards. They are also kingly because they govern in accordance with law whereas tyrants are typically unrestrained by laws. The third species is the *aesymnetia* or 'dictatorship' which existed at an earlier time in Greek history. It is an elective tyranny similar to the previous type, the barbarian monarchy, in that the *aesymnetes* rules according to law, but different because he is elected rather than hereditary. The position could be held for life or for much shorter periods. Like the barbarian kingship it is tyrannical because it is despotic but kingly because its subjects consent to it. The fourth species of kingship is associated with the heroic age. Unlike the previous two it does not have any tyrannical characteristics. Such kings were hereditary and ruled according to law over willing subjects. Originally their control was unlimited, except presumably by law, but they gradually lost their powers until, in some states, they were left with nothing but certain religious functions. Aristotle defines this type of kingship in terms of an intermediate stage in its evolution when its powers were limited but still substantial. This sort of king is a general and a judge and has control of religion. The fifth type is absolute kingship (*pambasileia*), the rule of one man who controls everything.

[40] III.14.vii (1285 ^{a} 27–9) 136; cf. IV.10.iv (1295 ^{a} 22–3) 170.

[41] V.10.ix (1311 ^{a} 4–5) 218.

[42] III.14.vii (1285 ^{a} 24–7) 136; V.10.x (1311 ^{a} 7–8) 218.

[43] *Rhetoric* I.8 (1366 ^{a} 6).   [44] III.14.

[45] III.15.ii (1286 ^{a} 2–5) 138–9.

Aristotle compares his rule to that of the head of a household by which he probably means that the absolute king has total and unfettered control over his community in the same way as the head of the household is complete master of all the members of his household. Such a person will be superior to any law and his rule may therefore be described as 'absolute' though the Greek word *pambasileia* refers not so much to freedom from legal restraint as to the all-embracing nature of such rule.

After listing the five different types Aristotle says that only the first, the Spartan type, and the last, absolute kingship, deserve further consideration.[46] The Spartan kingship is an important type of generalship and absolute kingship as we shall see is of interest for theoretical and philosophical reasons. In general, however, Aristotle, whose early career owed much to the patronage of monarchs, looks on kingship as a type of government belonging to a more primitive stage of political development, represented by the barbarians and the early Greeks, and not appropriate for contemporary Greek states.

Aristotle's account of the species of tyranny is very perfunctory.[47] He mentions only three, two of which are identical with the second and third species of kingship, the barbaric kingship and the *aesymnetia*, both of which are partly kingly and partly tyrannical. Having merely summarized his previous account of these two, he then describes the third type which is the extreme or pure type of tyranny. It is the counterpart of absolute kingship, combining all the essential characteristics of tyranny: irresponsibility, selfishness, violence.

Aristocracy

Aristocracy ('rule by the best men') is originally defined as rule by a few in the common interest. As its name implies, it gives power to the 'best' men and its basic principle is virtue or 'merit' (*axia*).[48] True aristocracies are governed by men who are truly or absolutely virtuous; the virtue of the good man and of the good citizen are identical.[49] Aristotle's account of ideal aristocracy raises difficult problems of interpretation. First, what is the relation of such aristocracy to absolute kingship? Aristocracy is sometimes coupled with kingship as one of the two best consitutions where the truly virtuous rule, and the only difference between it and ideal kingship seems to be in the size of the ruling group.[50] Because the ideal kingship described by Aristotle is absolute

---

[46] III.15.i (1285 b 33–5) 138.   [47] IV.10.   [48] III.5.v (1278 a 18–20) 112.
[49] IV.7.ii (1293 b 1–7) 165.
[50] III.15.x (1286 b 3–7) 140; III.18.i (1288 a 32–41) 147; IV.2.i (1289 a 31–3) 151.

kingship, it would seem that ideal aristocracy is the absolute rule of a
few outstanding men, whose virtue is similarly incomparable with that
of other members of the community. But, though Aristotle mentions
the possibility of absolute rule by more than one man,[51] he also describes
aristocracy as a type of political rule[52] which implies that the rulers in
an aristocracy are not as powerful or outstanding as absolute rulers.
Secondly, when Aristotle says at the beginning of Book Four that he
has already discussed ideal aristocracy to what is he referring?[53] Is it
the aristocracy briefly mentioned in Book Three? Is it the ideal state
described in Books Seven and Eight, in which case these books should
perhaps be placed, as many editors have placed them, before Book Four?
Is he referring to a section on ideal aristocracy which was in an earlier
version of the *Politics* but has been lost from the text that has come
down to us?

These questions cannot be answered with certainty. It is safest to
assume that Aristotle himself did not have a consistent view of the
precise nature of the ideal aristocracy. Its essential characteristic is that
it is rule by the truly virtuous few and he would probably have described
both political rule and absolute rule by such men as aristocratic. The
ideal state of Books Seven and Eight, though not explicitly described as
an aristocracy, does, as we shall see, fit the general description of aristocracy. But the order of books need not therefore be changed. The
references in Book Three to the rule of the few best men, whether
absolute or political, are quite sufficient to explain Aristotle's statement
at the beginning of Book Four that he has already dealt with aristocracy.
There is certainly no need to suppose the existence of a lost treatise
or section on aristocracy.

The term 'aristocracy' was also commonly used to refer to constitutions which fell short of the ideal type, which Aristotle describes as
'so-called aristocracies'. Their main characteristic is that they incorporate
virtue or merit as a distributive principle. The virtue and merit, however,
are not the same as those found in the best form of aristocracy. The
good men in a so-called aristocracy are merely those who are considered
virtuous in their community and they are not in Aristotle's opinion
truly good. Their virtue is relative to the constitution not absolute.[54]
They are described as 'nobles'[55] and usually possess the attributes of

[51]   III.13.xiii–xiv (1284 a 3–15) 132.
[52]   III.17.iv (1288 a 9–11) 146.
[53]   IV.2.i (1289 a 30–1) 151; cf. IV.7.ii (1293 b 1–3) 165.
[54]   IV.7.ii (1293 b 6–7) 165.
[55]   e.g. IV.8.iv (1293 b 38–40) 166; V.8.xvii (1309 a 2–3) 212.

education or 'culture'[56] and noble birth. They have the characteristics which a modern reader would normally associate with the idea of aristocracy: inherited wealth and status combined with a certain degree of general culture and education.

Aristotle briefly describes three species of so-called aristocracy, all of which are mixed constitutions and employ other principles besides virtue.[57] The first species combines virtue with wealth and numbers as in Carthage. The second, of which Sparta is an example, combines only two principles, virtue and the democratic principle of freedom. The third includes those varieties of the polity which 'incline more to oligarchy.' As the polity combines the oligarchic and democratic principles of wealth and freedom, this third type presumably consists of those constitutions which combine wealth and freedom but give a preponderant weight to wealth. But what makes this an aristocracy? Aristotle tries to justify such a description by saying that education and good birth 'belong more to the well-to-do';[58] the wealthy, that is, tend to have aristocratic qualities. This implies, however, that all oligarchies are aristocratic and tends to undermine Aristotle's original reason for introducing the category of so-called aristocracy which was to distinguish such constitutions from oligarchies.

Aristotle does not mention any constitutions which are based solely on this relative type of virtue. There are, that is, no so-called aristocracies which are purely aristocratic. His remarks on the Carthaginian constitution in Book Two suggest the theoretical possibility of such a constitution[59] but he does not follow this up later. The reason may lie in his belief that, apart from the ideal of rule by the absolutely best men, the best constitutions are mixed. The relatively best men, an aristocratic class such as existed in many Greek states, were not to be trusted with complete power. To describe their rule as the pure form of so-called aristocracy would imply, given that aristocracy is a normal or good type of constitution, that this was the best form of so-called aristocracy, whereas such an unmixed form is inferior to a constitution which also includes other principles such as wealth or freedom. So-called aristocracy thus becomes essentially a mixed constitution. This is confirmed in the account of the three elements of government where the institutional structures typical of aristocracy involve a balance between the exclusiveness of oligarchy and the equality of democracy.

[56] IV.15.x (1299 ^{b} 25) 184; *Rhetoric* I.8 (1365 ^{b} 34).
[57] IV.7.iv–v (1293 ^{b} 14–21) 165.
[58] IV.8.iii (1293 ^{b} 37–8) 166.
[59] e.g. II.11.viii (1273 ^{a} 21–5) 96.

The aristocratic device for selecting officials, for example, is to choose them by popular election which is a compromise between the democratic method of lot and the oligarchic method of selection by a few.[60] In general, the institutions are very similar to those of the polity. Indeed, in many respects so-called aristocracy is closer to the polity than to any other type of constitution and is best understood as a variety or offshoot of the polity.

Oligarchy

Oligarchy is a perverted constitution in which the few rule in their own interests. The dominant economic group is the wealthy and wealth is both the distributive principle of oligarchy and its goal. Though other characteristics besides wealth, for instance noble birth and education, may be associated with oligarchy they are not essential to it in the same way as wealth. They are accidental characteristics which often accompany wealth but need not; the rich who rule in an oligarchy may include wealthy artisans or tradesmen, men of low birth and little culture.[61] The fewness of the rulers is also an essential criterion of oligarchy. It marks the major difference between moderate oligarchy and the polity[62] and is the main means of distinguishing those arrangements of the three elements of government which are especially oligarchic. In the selection of magistrates, for example, the oligarchic method is for some (rather than for all) to appoint officials from some (rather than all).[63] Again, it is characteristic of the judicial process in oligarchies that all cases are tried by juries consisting of a few.[64]

Aristotle describes four types of oligarchy.[65] The first is the most moderate form which approaches the polity;[66] the rulers rule in accordance with law and access to office is determined by a property qualification which is not very restrictive. The qualification is set relatively low and office is open to all who can acquire the stated amount of property. In Book Six Aristotle recommends two separate property qualifications for this type; a high one for entry to the most important offices and a low one for 'lesser but essential offices'.[67] Presumably, however, even this lower qualification will be sufficiently restrictive to ensure that only a minority of the free men participate in political office and that the constitution deserves the name 'oligarchy'. The second type is more

[60] IV.15.xxi (1300 b 4–5) 186; cf. IV.5.i (1292 b 2–4) 161.
[61] III.5.vi (1278 a 21–5) 112.   [62] IV.13.vii (1297 b 2–6) 177.
[63] IV.15.xxi (1300 b 1–3) 186.   [64] IV.16.viii (1301 a 12–13) 188.
[65] IV.5–6; VI.6.   [66] VI.6.i (1320 b 21–2) 247.
[67] VI.6.ii (1320 b 23–5) 247.

exclusive. Qualification for office is higher and new appointments are made by those already holding office. In general, the rulers are fewer and richer than in the moderate oligarchy though they still rule in accordance with law and are therefore not entirely self-interested. The third type is narrower still and includes the further restriction that membership of the governing class is hereditary. Finally, the fourth type contains an even smaller and richer class which now rules without the control of laws. This is the pure or unmixed form of oligarchy, described as *dynasteia*, the Greek term for rule by a powerful family or families.[68] This typology is very schematic. Aristotle has taken the essential characteristics of oligarchy, such as wealth, fewness and self-interestedness, and constructed a set of categories ranging from the pure type in which all these characteristics exist in their extreme form to the moderate type which is only just oligarchic and shades off into the polity.

Democracy

Of the three types of perverted constitution, Aristotle gives most attention to democracy. It had been the prevailing form of government in Athens for over a century and had evolved a compelling set of principles and ideals which he felt bound to analyse and criticize in some detail. The literal meaning of 'democracy' is rule by the *demos* or 'people' which in Greek can refer either to the whole people, that is all those with some rights of citizenship, or to one section of the citizens, the 'common people' as distinct from the nobility or the rich. Like most critics of democracy, Aristotle understands it in the more restricted sense as rule by the 'common people'; it is the rule of the majority and the poor.[69] The characteristic principle of democracy is freedom which has two elements:[70] first, free birth is the democratic qualification for citizenship rights; secondly, freedom, in the sense of 'living as one likes', is the end or goal of democracy. The belief that political participation should depend on free birth is closely connected with the democratic principle of equality. The democrat believes in equal shares for all ('arithmetic' equality in Aristotle's terminology) which leads to a belief in the supremacy of the majority. Because democracy is essentially rule by the majority rather than rule by all it is quite compatible with the restriction of the rights of minorities. Even when the rights of minorities are not formally restricted, the normal result of giving the right of

[68] IV.5.ii (1292 ^{b} 9–10) 161.   [69] IV.4.vi (1290 ^{b} 17–19) 155.
[70] VI.2.i–iv (1317 ^{a} 40–^{b} 17) 236–7.

participation to all free men will be the domination of the government
by a cohesive majority, the *demos*.

The typically democratic ways of organizing the elements of government are derived from the belief in equality. The democratic method of
deliberation is for all to deliberate about all matters.[71] Similarly, the
democratic judicial method is for all cases to be decided by juries drawn
from all the people.[72] In order to ensure that everyone is able to
participate without financial loss, democracies institute payment for
attendance at the assembly and for performing other political duties.
Magistracies are open to everyone and where possible the selection is
made by lot rather than election. To discourage officials from acquiring
too much power democracies tend to make the length of tenure brief
and to restrict the right of reappointment.

Aristotle describes four main types of democracy[73] which, like the
types of oligarchy, follow a progression from the moderate to the extreme. The first, moderate, democracy will involve some sort of property
qualification for officials. The people, being predominantly agricultural,
will have little time to spend on public affairs and will be happy to
leave many of the decisions to the officials who will be elected from the
nobility.[74] Government will be conducted within the limits of established
law. Aristotle prefers an agricultural populace not because farmers are
more politically capable than other types of worker but because they
are less ambitious and more docile. The second type is similar except
that there is no property qualification for officials and the right to hold
office is now given to all who are not disqualified by birth. However,
because no payment is made for performing public duties, the bulk of
the population still cannot afford to spend time on politics. Government
is carried on under law. In the third type, the citizenship qualification
is further relaxed to include all free men, including, presumably, such
people as aliens and children of emancipated slaves who would be
excluded in the first two types. The social composition of the citizen
body is also less rural and more urban. In extreme democracy, all
restraints have disappeared. An increase in the public revenues allows
payment for political participation. A predominantly urban people is
now able to give all its time to politics with the result that government
is by popular decree, unrestrained by law, and is directed wholly
towards the interests of the poor. This type of democracy is analagous
to the extreme form of tyranny in both its self-interestedness and its

[71] IV.14.iv (1298 a 9–10) 179.   [72] IV.16.viii (1301 a 11–12) 188.
[73] IV.4; IV.6; VI.4.   [74] VI.4.vi (1318 b 32–6) 241.

lawlessness. It is susceptible to the influence of the demagogue who stands in the same relation to the popular assembly as the flatterer does to the tyrant.

Aristotle's first account of the types of democracy includes five types. The additional type, which he puts first, is a constitution where all are really equal and where the poor have no more power than the rich.

In such the law lays down that the poor shall not enjoy any advantage over the rich, that neither class shall dominate the other but both shall be exactly similar. For if, as is generally held, freedom is especially to be found in democracy, and also equality, this condition is best realized when all share in equal measure the whole constitution. But since the people are the more numerous class and the decision of the majority prevails, such a constitution must be a democracy.[75]

Aristotle is thus aware that the principles of democracy, especially equality, need not necessarily lead to the domination of the majority but can justify the protection of the liberty of all. However, he does not include this type in his subsequent accounts of the types of democracy. It is sometimes thought to have been incorporated into the first of the other four, the most moderate type of democracy, or to have been dropped because it does not fit well with the other, supposedly more realistic, types. But neither of these explanations is satisfactory. The 'extra' type is unlike the moderate democracy. Though it is also an admirable type of democracy, it is valuable not because democratic principles are blunted and compromised in it but because it implements these principles in an ideal way. Nor can it have been suppressed simply because it is abstract or unrealistic. The fourth type, 'extreme' democracy, is essentially an ideal abstraction and the characteristics and order of the other, less 'pure', types are determined primarily by theoretical rather than historical considerations. The most likely reason for the suppression of the extra type is that it upsets the theoretical pattern of Aristotle's analysis of democracy. Democracy is a perverted constitution and, as with the other special types of perverted constitution, oligarchy and tyranny, the ideal or pure type must be the worst because it carries bad principles to their extremes. To admit another pure type of democracy which could be said to be the best type would compromise Aristotle's whole theory of the nature of democracy and of its relation to other general types, especially oligarchy and polity.

[75] IV.4.xxii–xxiii (1291 ^{b} 31–8) 159.

Polity

The Greek language in Aristotle's day possessed generally accepted words for the good and bad forms of the rule of one and of the few. 'Democracy' however, was the only term regularly used for rule of the many. Once it had been preempted for the bad form, Aristotle was left with the problem of naming the good form. In the *Ethics*, he prefers 'timocracy'[76] but in the *Politics* he adopts the more neutral *politeia*, which is also the general word for constitution. *Politeia* is traditionally translated as 'polity' when it refers to this specific type of constitution and as 'constitution' when it refers to constitutions in general. But we should not forget that Aristotle uses the same word for both and that sometimes it is not clear whether he intends the general or the specific sense. Polity is initially defined as the rule of the many in the common interest,[77] and is then described as the rule of those bearing arms.[78] Later it is a mixture of oligarchy and democracy[79] and is identified with rule by the middle class.[80]

These different descriptions of the polity are not all completely consistent. First, if the polity is a mixture or balance between oligarchy and democracy it is not necessarily a form of majority rule any more than it is a form of minority rule. This ambivalence appears when Aristotle says both that a polity must be describable equally as a democracy and as an oligarchy[81] and also that mixtures of oligarchy and democracy that incline towards oligarchy are called aristocracies while those that incline towards democracy are called polities.[82] Secondly, there is an ambiguity in the description of the polity as a 'moderate' or 'middle' constitution. On the one hand, it means a mixed constitution which contains both oligarchic and democratic elements and institutions. On the other hand, it means a constitution which is a compromise between oligarchy and democracy but is not necessarily made up of oligarchic and democratic elements. When polity is described, for example, as rule of the middle class or those of moderate means, it is a moderate constitution but not, strictly speaking, a mixed constitution. The same ambiguity occurs, as we shall see, in Aristotle's arguments in favour of the superiority of the polity over oligarchy and democracy.

[76] *EN* VIII.10 (1160 ^{a} 33–5). [77] III.7.iii (1279 ^{a} 37–9) 116.
[78] III.7.iv (1279 ^{a} 40–^{b} 4) 116. [79] IV.8.iii (1293 ^{b} 33–4) 166.
[80] IV.11.ii–iii (1295 ^{a} 31–40) 171.
[81] IV.9.vi; x (1294 ^{b} 14–16; 34–6) 168–9.
[82] IV.3.vii (1290 ^{a} 16–19) 154; V.7.vi (1307 ^{a} 15–16) 207.

The general principle which governs the institutional structure of the polity is that it should provide a combination of oligarchic and democratic features. For example, to exercise the deliberative function there may be a popular assembly but its powers will be limited.[83] Again, some officials may be appointed oligarchically, others democratically[84] and the judicial functions are usually organized so that some juries are taken from all classes and some from certain classes only.[85] On the whole, however, Aristotle is not very definite about the institutional organization of the polity, probably because there is a variety of ways in which oligarchy and democracy may be combined. Moreover, so-called aristocracy is also a mixed constitution and Aristotle does not always clearly distinguish between the arrangements characteristic of aristocracy and those more appropriate to the polity.[86]

Though he has admitted that polities may be constructed in different ways, Aristotle does not give a formal typology of the polity. It is a constitution which has rarely if ever existed in its true form and is an abstract ideal which serves as a standard for the deviant forms of oligarchy and democracy. He does, however, describe the constitutions of certain cities as polities, on the grounds, presumably, that they are sufficiently close to the ideal polity to deserve the name. He also talks of types of polity which tend towards aristocracy or oligarchy or democracy. Thus the same pattern occurs as with the other major types of constitution; an ideal or pure type with subsidiary species containing elements or aspects of it.

[83] IV.14.xvi (1298 ^{b} 38–1299 ^{a} 1) 182.
[84] IV.15.xix–xx (1300 ^{a} 34–^{b} 1) 186.
[85] IV.16.viii (1301 ^{a} 13–15) 188.
[86] IV.14.x (1298 ^{b} 8–11) 180; IV.16.viii (1301 ^{a} 13–15) 188.

CHAPTER FIVE

THE RULE OF THE BEST MEN

We may now consider Aristotle's account of the relative merits of different constitutions, beginning with his views about the best possible constitution. The true purpose of the *polis* is the achievement of the good life and the best constitution will be one that realizes this purpose. Aristotle describes two types of best constitution, absolute rule and aristocracy in accordance with law. Though there are important differences between them, both are founded on the principle that in the best state the best men or the men of full virtue must rule. This principle is itself supported on two general grounds: first, that only the best men will be capable of governing the city in the best possible manner; second, that, quite apart from the good consequences of their rule, the best men deserve the honour of ruling.

The need for good rulers

That the best state will need the best government is a truism whatever view is taken of the role of government and law in the community. For Aristotle, however, it is especially important because of the crucial part played by the rulers and the laws in the achievement of the good life. The authoritarian role which he gives to government is partly the result of his view of ethical knowledge. He believes that the nature of virtue and happiness can be discovered and verified objectively, and that it is therefore possible to have rulers who know the right answers to ethical questions. Another factor is his theory of moral education. The development of an ethically virtuous disposition depends on acquiring the right habits of virtuous behaviour.[1] Fully virtuous action, it is true, implies more than simply performing the appropriate acts out of habit; one must know what one is doing and must have deliberately chosen to do it for its own sake.[2] But in moral development the external behaviour comes first; one must learn to do the right thing for the wrong reasons before one can do it for the right reasons. In most states the responsibility for instilling the right habits in the young has been left to individual families. But this method is unsatisfactory and the proper instrument

[1] VII.13.xi (1332 a 39–40) 284; *EN* X.9 (1179 b 20–1).
[2] *EN* II.4 (1105 a 28–33).

for maintaining virtue is the law.[3] The individual father does not have the same compulsive force and is more likely to antagonize than the impersonal and impartial commands of law. Furthermore, leaving moral education to individual families allows the head of each family to live as he pleases like the Cyclops in Homer's *Odyssey*, 'to his own wife and children dealing law'. This is likely to lead to social disunity and conflict and will prevent the city as a whole from achieving the common ideal of the good life. Aristotle does not mean that the family should have no role in education. As we have seen, he wants the household to continue as an important part of the *polis* and the head of the household, being the best judge of the particular characteristics of his own particular family, is to have immediate control over his wife, children, and slaves. Aristotle is merely concerned that the state should exercise general control over education in order to prevent conflict between the behaviour of individuals and the values of the community.

In order to make the citizens virtuous, it will be necessary not only to control the education of the young but also to supervise closely the whole of men's lives.

But surely it is not enough that when they are young they should get the right nurture and attention; since they must, even when they are grown up, practise and be habituated to them, we shall need laws for this as well and generally speaking to cover the whole of life, for most people obey necessity rather than argument and punishments rather than a sense of what is noble.[4]

Indeed, Aristotle seems to consider that the entire moral code of the ideal society will be included in the law. The intellectual virtues and philosophical contemplation will be subject to indirect control only; the state can provide the right conditions for their pursuit but will not be able to enforce them directly. But acts of ethical virtue can be publicly compelled. In his account of justice in the *Ethics*,[5] Aristotle equates universal justice, complete social virtue, with what is lawful; all ethically virtuous behaviour is to be enforced by the law. This identification of the lawful and the moral is facilitated by the Greek word for 'law', *nomos*. which covers not only laws in the sense of statutes passed by legislative bodies but also any shared rule of social behaviour, such as unwritten customs and conventions. Following Greek usage, Aristotle includes unwritten as well as written 'laws' among the means at the statesman's disposal[6] and 'legal' control is thus control exercised

---

[3] *EN* X.9 (1180 a 18–b 7).   [4] *EN* X.9 (1180 a 1–5).
[5] *EN* V.1.   [6] *EN* X.9 (1180 b 1); VI.5.ii (1319 b 40) 244.

through the manipulation of custom and convention as well as by means of written statutes. Not all Greeks were as authoritarian as Aristotle and not all Greek states actually enforced all their social conventions. In most states, particularly the more liberal ones like democratic Athens, there would be traditional customs which would be treated as personal or family matters and would not be enforced by the institutions of the state. Yet, because any norm that was called a *nomos* carried thereby the implication that it was publicly binding and could legitimately be enforced through the courts, there was no clear distinction between law and morality and no area of behaviour which was clearly beyond the scope of the legal and political institutions. It was therefore conceptually much easier to argue for, rather than against, the legal enforcement of morality. Complete control of the moral behaviour of a community would not seem impracticable to Aristotle. The Greek city state was small in size and its members, like members of all small communities, were especially susceptible to the influences of informal group pressures. The Spartans, whose public concern for education Aristotle much admires,[7] though he does not agree altogether with their values,[8] had achieved a remarkable degree of social and ideological conformity through a combination of legal and institutional control and social pressure. In the light of this example, the ideal of complete political control of morality must have seemed not only attractive but also quite attainable, provided only that those in power were truly virtuous and wise.

The need to provide good government is not the only reason why the best men should rule. Even if they could not provide a better type of government they would still deserve to be in a position of power because distributive justice demands that their ethical and intellectual superiority be accorded a corresponding superiority in the state. Aristotle assumes, together with most Greeks, that political office is a species of 'honour' (*time*) and is of inherent value to those who possess it. Being of value, it ought to be distributed justly. He discusses the application of distributive justice to the distribution of political power in Book Three, beginning with the conflict between oligarchic and democratic principles.[9] With typical respect for convictions which are widely held he admits that both oligarchs and democrats have grasped

---

[7] *EN* X.9 (1180 a 24–6).

[8] II.9.xxxiv–xxxv (1271 b 2–10) 90; VII.2.ix (1324 b 5–9) 259-60; VII.15.vi (1334 a 40–b 3) 290–1.

[9] III.9; 12.

part of the truth. The democrats rightly recognize that equality is just but they ignore the qualification that it is just only for those who ought to be considered equals. Oligarchs, on the other hand, recognize that inequality can be just, but they too ignore the qualification that it is just only for those who should be considered unequal.[10] The fundamental question which both sides fail to deal with satisfactorily is who is to count as equal or unequal and the answer to it lies in the nature of the job to be done or the end to be pursued. In more modern terms, any discrimination or lack of discrimination must be justified in terms of relevant criteria. For example, it is just to exclude people from playing a particular sport on the grounds of inferior athletic ability but not on the grounds of race or colour. Aristotle uses the example of flute players.[11] The best flutes are given to the best flute players not to those who are nobly born even if noble birth itself is thought to be a better quality than the ability to play the flute. The sole consideration must be ability at the work which has to be done, in this case flute-playing. When distributing honour and power within the state, we must therefore look to the function or purpose of the state. The state exists not just for the sake of mere existence but also for the purpose of the good life. The criteria of the oligarch and the democrat, wealth and free birth, are relevant to the existence of the state (for the state must have some wealth and cannot be made up of slaves) but they overlook the achievement of the good life which is the paramount end.[12] The men of 'civic virtue', on the other hand, do contribute to this end.[13] As rulers they will be capable, as we have seen, of instilling virtue into their fellow citizens. More important, simply by being men of virtue they are helping to fulfil the highest purpose of the *polis*. The *polis* aims at the good life and so those who achieve the good life are realizing this aim. The claim of the virtuous thus depends both on their ability to rule well and on their participation in the end of the state.

Though Aristotle says that virtue is the most important criterion it is not the only one. Criteria such as wealth, freedom, and good birth are insufficient on their own but are not rejected altogether. The democrat and the oligarch are only partially, not completely, mistaken; they each recognize one of the proper criteria but ignore the others. The continuing, though subordinate, value of these other criteria has important consequences for the nature of the best constitution. The best state will be

---

[10] III.9.i–iv (1280 ^{a} 9–25) 118–19.
[11] III.12.iv–v (1282 ^{b} 31–1283 ^{a} 1) 128.
[12] III.9.v–vi (1280 ^{a} 25–32) 119.   [13] III.9.xv (1281 ^{a} 4–8) 121.

one where government is in the hands of men of 'virtue endowed with material good',[14] men who possess all the qualities which contribute to the purpose of the *polis*. But if different qualities are possessed by different groups, Aristotle's argument suggests that power will have to be shared between them. His account of distributive justice and the distribution of power thus looks forward both to the ideal rule of those who have truly achieved the good life and also to the theory that the second-best constitution will be a mixed constitution.

In his initial classification of constitutions, Aristotle describes three types of 'correct' or 'normal' constitution, kingship, aristocracy, and polity, depending on whether government is in the hands of one man, the few or the many. We might therefore expect that there are three types of rule of the best. However, he later claims that there are only two constitutions, kingship and aristocracy, in which rule is entrusted to those who combine full virtue with the necessary material equipment. Polity has been excluded because it is most unlikely that more than a few will be capable of obtaining perfect virtue; military virtue is the best to which a majority may aspire.[15] Aristotle offers no justification for this opinion and feels that none is necessary. The good life, as he conceives it, requires a reasonable amount of wealth, education and leisure and is necessarily restricted to a small proportion of the population.

The ideal kingship and aristocracy in which the truly virtuous rule may each take two different forms, depending on whether the rulers govern absolutely or in accordance with law. Of the two types of ideal rule under law, only aristocracy is discussed at any length. This is the ideal state described in Books Seven and Eight which, though not explicitly called an aristocracy, does, as we shall see, come within Aristotle's definition of ideal aristocracy. Ideal kingship in accordance with law is not one of the types of kingship singled out by Aristotle as worthy of special attention and receives only passing mention.[16] Absolute rule, however, both of one man and a few, is seriously considered. Though Aristotle discusses it within the context of kingship, his account is not meant to be restricted to a single ruler; the possibility of absolute rule by more than one man is clearly envisaged.

Absolute Rule and the Rule of Law

Though the discussion of absolute rule is brief, it is of considerable

---

[14] IV.2.i (1289 a 31–3) 151.

[15] III.7.iv (1279 a 39–b 2) 116.   [16] e.g. III.15.

significance in Aristotle's political theory. The main characteristics of the absolute ruler have already been described: he is all-powerful and can decide any issue on the basis of his own judgement without being bound by any law; he may still use law as an instrument of social control so long as he himself is not bound by any of his laws and can change them at will. In what circumstances, if any, is absolute rule justified? The starting-point for Aristotle's discussion is Plato's argument in the *Statesman* that absolute rule is superior to the rule of law. According to Plato, laws are necessarily general in their application and because of the variety of human situations cannot deal accurately and correctly with every possible situation. In contrast, the truly skilled ruler, with scientific knowledge of the art of ruling, will always, like the skilled doctor, know the correct prescription for any particular occasion. No one would expect a doctor to be bound by instructions that he has previously given. Similarly, the ideal statesman must not be bound by any existing law. The best form of constitution is therefore one where all power is in the hands of a truly skilled ruler or rulers, whose discretion is not restricted by any previously established laws.

Though Plato holds that the rule of the true statesman is preferable to a regime which adheres strictly to a legal code, he also argues that, in the absence of a true statesman, government in accordance with a legal code is preferable to a system which allows discretion to those in power. Men who are not truly wise will use such discretion not for the purposes of justice but in their own self-interest. The anomalies caused by a legal code are more tolerable than the consistent injustice which will result from placing ordinary men in a position of unlimited power. Plato's conclusion, which he repeats in the *Laws*, is that government in accordance with law is inferior to the unrestrained rule of the truly wise statesman but superior to the unrestrained rule of ordinary men.

Aristotle accepts Plato's arguments but he also supplements and modifies them in certain important respects. Rather than begin with his account of absolute rule, it may be more useful to look first at his attitude towards rule in accordance with law. The arguments in favour of the rule of law in the *Politics*[17] are said to be the arguments given by 'those who dispute about kingship'[18] and Aristotle does not explicitly vouch for them himself. Though they contain much with which he would agree, they should not be used as independent evidence of his views. To discover his attitude to law we need to begin elsewhere,

[17] III. 15–16.
[18] III.16.xiii (1287 b 35–6) 145; cf. III.15.iii (1286 a 6–7)·139.

in particular with certain passages in the *Rhetoric* and the *Ethics*. He accepts Plato's argument that law is deficient because of its generality. Any law, because it is formulated in general terms, is bound to be mistaken or found wanting in certain particular situations. In such cases, it will need correction or supplementation with reference to

what the legislator himself would have said had he been present and would have put in his law had he known.[19]

Aristotle seems to acknowledge more readily than Plato that the exercise of such discretion is an inescapable feature of all government including government in accordance with law. Those who administer the law must always, to some extent, be involved in creating the law. But he shares Plato's mistrust of ordinary men in positions of power and wants to restrict their discretion as far as possible. In the *Rhetoric* he gives three reasons for limiting discretion in the administration of law.

First, to find one man, or a few men, who are sensible persons and capable of legislating and administering justice is easier than to find a large number. Next laws are made after long consideration, whereas decisions in the courts are given at short notice, which makes it hard for those who try the case to satisfy the claims of justice and expediency. The weightiest reason of all is that the decision of the law-giver is not particular but prospective and general, whereas members of the assembly and the jury find it their duty to decide on definite cases brought before them. They will often have allowed themselves to be so much influenced by feelings of friendship or hatred or self-interest that they lose any clear vision of the truth and have their judgment obscured by considerations of personal pleasure or pain.[20]

Of these reasons, the first, that a large body cannot deliberate as well as a small one, applies only to states such as Athens where law-drafting was assigned to a small group while the administration of law was handled by large, popular juries. The second and third reasons, however, are of wider application. They turn on the fallibility of the juror or judge, his inability to decide a complex issue in a short time and his susceptibility to emotions and to considerations of self-interest. The self-interest of the judge is also referred to in the *Ethics*:

we do not allow men to rule . . . because a man behaves in his own self-interest and becomes a tyrant.[21]

Similarly, in the *Politics*, Aristotle concentrates on the partiality and

---

[19] *EN* V.10 (1137 ^{b} 22–4).
[20] *Rhetoric* I.1 (1354 ^{a} 34– ^{b} 11).   [21] *EN* V.6 (1134 ^{a} 35– ^{b} 1).

emotions which affect the decisions of individual human beings but are absent from the law[22] and describes the contrast between passionate man and dispassionate law in the famous epigram 'law is intellect without desire.'[23] Thus for Aristotle, as for Plato, the rule of law is preferable to the rule of corruptible and fallible men. It may be impossible to have a pure rule of law where everything is covered by law and nothing is left to human discretion, but this is the ideal towards which one should aim in a world of imperfect men.

Aristotle's justification of law, unlike Plato's, does not depend wholly on human weakness. He has another line of argument which makes use of the connected notions of equality, distributive justice, and political rule. Political power ought to be distributed in accordance with distributive justice. In the typical *polis*, the citizens will be either 'arithmetically' or 'proportionately' equal and therefore they will all deserve some share in political office. This is the type of rule which Aristotle describes as 'political' and which typically requires an alternation between ruling and being ruled. Such a distribution and alternation of political power will need to be conducted according to rules which will be laws of the constitution. A political community whose citizens are equal will therefore need to conduct its government in accordance with law.[24] Thus law is required not only by human fallibility and corruptibility but also by human equality. This is an important qualification because it implies that government in accordance with law is not necessarily inferior to absolute rule and it leads Aristotle to describe two forms of ideal government, one absolute, the other in accordance with law.

If law is required both by human fallibility and by equality, then absolute rule, rule without law, will be justified only when the ruler or rulers are both incorruptible and infallible and not even proportionately equal to the other members of the state. These are the conditions for absolute rule which may be inferred from Aristotle's arguments for law and which are confirmed by his account of the absolute ruler.

But if there is one man so superlatively excellent (or several but not enough to make the whole complement of a city) that the goodness and ability of all the rest are simply not to be compared with his (or theirs), such men we should not assume to be parts of the state at all. To judge them worthy of mere equality with the rest would be to

[22] III.15.v (1286 ^{a} 17–20) 139; III.16.v–ix (1287 ^{a} 27–^{b} 8) 143–4; cf. III.9.ii (1280 ^{a} 14–16) 118.

[23] III.16.v (1287 ^{a} 32) 143.

[24] *EN* V.6 (1134 ^{a} 26–30; ^{b} 13–15); cf. III.16.iii (1287 ^{a} 16–18) 143.

do them an unjustice, so far superior are they in virtue and political
capacity. We may fairly regard such a one as like a god among men. In
that case clearly legislation, the aim of which we have been discussing,
is not relevant, since legislation must refer to equals in birth and
capacity; and there is no law that can govern these exceptional men.
They are themselves law.[25]

The absolute ruler must be outstanding in both virtue and 'political
capacity', an imprecise phrase which presumably refers to the intellectual and material resources which such men will need if they are to dominate a state. Moreover, his virtue and capacity must be so outstanding
as not to be comparable with those of the rest of the community. The
concept of comparability is precise and important. Two things are
comparable, if they can be compared on the same scale as fractions of
one another or at least as greater than or less than or equal to one
another. Comparability is thus the essential condition for equality in
Aristotle's sense. Only if people's respective merits can be compared,
metaphorically if not literally, as fractions or as proportions of one
another can they be either arithmetically or proportionately equal. If the
absolute ruler's qualities are incomparable then he cannot be expected
to share his rule with his subjects and indeed he is perhaps hardly part
of the same city as they are.

Aristotle emphasizes the relative merits of the absolute ruler, his
superiority to others in the community, rather than his intrinsic merits,
his incorruptibility and wisdom. His arguments for the rule of law
lead us to expect that the intrinsic criterion will also be important.
If one of the reasons for law is the need to guard against the evil consequences of human fallibility and corruptibility, absolute rule cannot be
safe unless the rulers are infallible and incorruptible. But in his account
of absolute rule Aristotle does not directly specify the intrinsic
criterion. The statement that such men are themselves the law is vague
and obscure. It might mean that the absolute ruler has the rational and
impartial characteristics associated with the law. But, in another passage
where the same phrase is used, it seems to be simply an alternative
description of absolute rule; the absolute ruler does not rule under the
law but provides the law himself.[26] The statement that the absolute
ruler is like a god among men is essentially comparative, illustrating the
extent of difference between the absolute ruler and his subjects rather
than saying that he actually has divine powers. If the subjects were in
some sense brutish or sub-human, it might be possible for a ruler to

[25] III.13.xiii–xiv (1284 ^{a} 3–14) 132.
[26] III.17.ii (1288 ^{a} 3) 146.

have incomparable qualities and yet be not wholly devoid of ignorance or corruption. In a Greek context, however, the possibility of such sufficiently inferior citizens is unthinkable. Aristotle believes that the Greeks are a superior race of men and thus, as far as Greek politics are concerned, the relative criterion for absolute rule implies the intrinsic criterion. Because of the superior qualities of the ordinary Greek, anyone who meets the relative criterion will also meet the intrinsic criterion; for absolute rule over Greeks, only divine candidates need apply.

Is such a paragon possible? Aristotle does not believe so.[27] A god among men would, after all, be an anomaly of nature which Aristotle the biologist would not happily countenance. It is true that in his discussion of absolute kingship in Book Three he does not deny the practical possibility of absolute rule. But he does not affirm it either. The discussion in Book Three is purely hypothetical; if there were such a man, then we ought to obey him gladly. Nothing that Aristotle says leads one to believe that justifiable absolute rule for Greeks was anything more than a theoretical possibility. He cannot have meant the account of the absolute ruler as a description of his former pupil, Alexander the Great; he would not have considered Alexander to be divine or quasi-divine. But this does not mean that he did not have Alexander in mind as he was writing. He may have been thinking of Alexander as a ruler who claimed the right to rule absolutely over Greeks without possessing the necessary personal qualities. The account of the absolute ruler can be a standard for judging actual rulers without being a description of any actual ruler; political ideals need not be irrelevant to everyday politics because they do not describe any existing political situation.

The account of absolute rule is an integral part of Aristotle's political theory because it is a necessary corollary of his attitude to the rule of law and political equality. His belief that the discretion of rulers should be limited by law does not apply to all conceivable societies. Like most of human weakness. If men were not emotional or partial, this justifications about human nature. Law is valuable, in part, because of the fact of human weakness. If men were not emotional or partial, thus justification of law would not hold good. Similarly, political rule and the interchange of ruler and ruled depend on the existence of a certain degree of human equality. If men were not sufficiently equal there would be no

---

[27] VII.14.iii (1332 ^{b} 22–7) 285.

justification for political rule under law. The incomparable, godlike paragon provides the limiting case, the case where alternation of ruler and ruled is inappropriate and where the rulers may have unfettered discretion. To expect Aristotle to have rejected absolute rule altogether, even as a theoretical possibility, would be asking him to abandon the principle that the nature of the best constitution for any community will depend on the particular qualities of its population. This belief in the essential relativism of constitutional arrangements is an important part of his general approach to political science and the recognition that absolute rule is justifiable in certain imaginable circumstances is a consequence of it. He reminds us that the constitutional principles we cherish are to be cherished because they work in the sort of society in which we have to live and not because they are appropriate for every conceivable society.

Ideal Aristocracy

The ideal state to which Aristotle gives the most attention is an aristocracy where the citizens are in some sense equal and where the government is carried on under law. This state is described in the last two books of the *Politics*, Books Seven and Eight, and is similar in many ways to the state described in Plato's *Laws*. The state of Plato's *Laws*, however, is definitely a second-best state, designed for a community which does not have members who are true statesmen. For Aristotle, on the other hand, aristocracy under the law is not necessarily inferior to absolute rule. Because he stipulated a relative as well as an intrinsic criterion for absolute rule, absolute rule is to be rejected not only in the absence of ideally virtuous and knowledgeable rulers but also when there is no one sufficiently superior to the rest of the community. Ideal aristocracy under the law results less from any deficiencies in the leaders of the community than from the assumption that there are people sufficiently numerous and similar to form a citizen body of equals. Aristotle's general attitude towards his ideal state is also different from Plato's. On several occasions, he reveals an impatience with minor points of organization[28] which contrasts sharply with Plato's almost inexhaustible ingenuity and concern for detail in the *Laws*. His account is also incomplete. Book Eight breaks off in the middle of a discussion of music in education. The description of ideal aristocracy may have been completed and subsequently lost, but because there are no refer-

[28] VII.5.ii (1326 ^{b} 32–6) 266–7; VII.12.ix (1331 ^{b} 18–23) 281.

ences in the *Politics* or elsewhere to material which might belong to a continuation of Book Eight, it is more likely that Aristotle gave up where our text finishes. The detailed description of an ideal state seems to have held little interest for him. He criticizes some of the details in the ideal states of Plato and others, thus supplementing the critique of ideal states in Book Two. Otherwise, his main concern is with general principle and method. He begins with a discussion of the purpose of the *polis* and the nature of the good life and it is noticeable how much of his discussion of particular aspects of the ideal state is conducted with direct and explicit reference to these first principles. His purpose seems to be not so much to provide a detailed blueprint for an ideal state as to emphasize and illustrate the proper method to be used when planning one. Once the general principles have been established and the method of applying these principles to individual problems has been demonstrated, then the details can safely be left to others who have more time and inclination for such work.

In the opening section on the good life[29] Aristotle summarizes certain conclusions from the ethical treatises and discusses the relative merits of the lives of the philosopher and the statesman. His main purpose is political rather than ethical:[30] he wants to show that the ideal state will not aim at unlimited wealth or domination over a few states. Comparing the state with the individual he argues that certain features of the good life for individuals also belong to the good life for states. Wealth and power are ignoble goals for whole communities as well as for individuals;[31] just as philosophical contemplation is the highest form of human activity, so states should prefer to live in peace and relative isolation from their neighbours.[32] In this section Aristotle adopts a slightly different attitude to the relation of individual good to the good of the whole state. In the *Ethics* he seems to imply a simple identity between the good of the state and the good of the individuals in it; the good of the state consists in its citizens' achieving their own individual happiness. Here, however, the relation is one of analogy rather than identity. But Aristotle still believes the good of the state cannot be achieved unless its members achieve their individual good.[33] The happiness of the state is not so distinct from the happiness of its members that the state can be happy without having individual members who are happy. This point is made most emphatically in Book Two, where

---

[29] VII.1–3.   [30] VII.2.iv (1324 a 19–23) 259.
[31] VII.1.   [32] VII.2–3.
[33] VII.2.v (1324 a 23–5) 259; VII.9.vii (1329 a 22–4) 274.

Aristotle criticizes Plato for depriving the class of guardians of happiness while insisting that the whole state should be happy.

> But it is impossible for the whole to be happy, unless the majority, if not actually all, or at any rate some, parts possess happiness. The evenness of an even number is a very different thing from the happiness of a city; two odd numbers added together make an even number, but two unhappy sections do not add up to a happy city.[34]

An even number may be made up of two odd numbers but two unhappy individuals cannot make a happy pair. The good of the state must therefore include the good of its individual members. The result of this discussion, then, is to supplement rather than replace the account of the aim of political science which is given in the *Ethics*. As well as trying to achieve human happiness for individual members of the community, which will still, no doubt, be the major part of its purpose, political science will have certain additional objectives for the community as a whole. For example, it will need to make the state peaceful rather than belligerent and self-sufficient rather than dependent on other states.

Aristotle describes his ideal state as being 'what one could wish for' (*kat'euchen*), but he is careful to insist that it requires nothing which is impossible.[35] When imagining an ideal state one may suppose that the state enjoys every good fortune but one cannot require anything which is contrary to nature, a limitation which some philosophers and political theorists have not recognized.[36] Any craftsman must have raw materials to work on and will not do his best work unless he has the best possible materials to begin with. The same applies to the legislator. His principal raw materials are men and territory and he must have the best possible if he wishes to construct an ideal state. The first question to be decided about the population is its proper size.[37] Aristotle does not give a precise number as Plato had done in the *Laws*. As we have seen, such precision of detail is not his main concern. Starting from the need to consider the function of the city, he argues that the number to be decided is not that of the total population but only that of the true members of the city, those who share in the good life of the city. If there are not enough citizens the city will not provide the necessities of life; if there are too many, the city will not be able to be governed well. It is very difficult to impose order on a large number of citizens. Moreover, if the citizens

---

[34] II.5.xxvii (1264 b 17–22) 67.
[35] VII.4.ii (1325 b 38–40) 264.
[36] Cf. II.6.vii (1265 a 17–18) 69.   [37] VII.4.

are to share in the governing of the city by appointing magistrates and judging disputes, they must be able to know the worth of their fellow citizens. Aristotle does not insist that all the decisions should be made by all the citizens. To be practicable this would require a community too small to provide the necessities of life. He will not completely sacrifice the economic and cultural advantages of size for the sake of maximizing individual political participation. Instead he strikes a balance. He accepts the necessity for specialized political functions and is ready to delegate some decision-making to various boards and officials provided the individual citizens can retain general control by making the major deliberative and judicial decisions.

He also considers the racial composition of the population of the best state.[38] Greeks are the only people capable of achieving an ideal community. They are superior to two other major racial groups. The first are the people of 'Europe', the colder regions to the north of Greece. These people are full of spirit but lacking in intelligence and skill. Consequently, they remain free but 'have no political organization' (*apoliteuta*), which probably means that they have no communities of the *polis* type.[39] They are also unable to rule their neighbours. The second group are the people of Asia who, conversely, have intelligence and skill but no spirit. They therefore remain enslaved to their rulers as the subjects of despotic governments. Only the Greeks, who occupy a middle place between these two groups, have both spirit and intelligence and are capable of living in a political community of free men. Indeed, says Aristotle in an enigmatic statement, if they could 'achieve one constitution' they would be capable of ruling everyone.[40] He seems here to envisage a political unity of the Greeks which could lead to world domination. But what sort of unity does he mean? A federation of cities or a national constitution transcending that of the *polis*? No clear answer can be given. We should not, however, make too much of this remark. It is in the nature of an aside and does not seriously qualify his conviction that the traditional Greek *polis* is the best form of political community.

Aristotle's belief in the racial superiority of the Greeks has already been mentioned in connection with his theory of natural slavery. Such a belief was common in his time and, though there were some who denied it, no moral opprobrium was attached to its expression. Considering how much his conception of the good life owes to Greek values

[38] VII.7.   [39] VII.7.ii (1327 b 26) 269.
[40] VII.7.iii (1327 b 31–3) 269.

and institutions, it was inevitable that he should think that Greeks were the people most capable of achieving it. Where he goes wrong is in attributing their greater propensity for his type of good life wholly to genetic rather than to cultural and environmental factors. His theory of racial differences was probably influenced by certain writers, notably the author of the Hippocratic treatise, *Airs, Waters, Places,* who traced the differences between races to differences of geography and climate. But there is no suggestion that, for him at any rate, the differences are purely environmental. They are natural differences and therefore innate and inevitable.[41] A similar concern for the right genetic qualities in the citizen population influences his attitude towards marriage and childbirth.[42] They are to be regulated to ensure that the children produced have the best possible natural characteristics. The age at which people marry and have children is to be controlled, partly in order to provide the right distance in time between the generations, but also to ensure that the best progeny are produced. Aristotle believes, from his biological studies, that the offspring of very young persons are inferior and this lends support to his view that men should not marry and have children till the age of thirty-seven, while women should marry at eighteen. To protect the natural quality of the citizen body he also argues that deformed children should not be allowed to survive but should be exposed. He is opposed, however, to the practice, not unknown in Greece, of exposing physically normal children simply for reasons of population control. Admittedly some sort of population control will be necessary; if the achievement of the good life depends on having an initial citizen population of the right size it will also depend on maintaining this population within due limits and Aristotle criticizes both Plato[43] and Phaleas[44] for neglecting this requirement. None the less, he opposes the exposure of surplus healthy children and prefers to rely on abortion before the embryo has acquired 'life and sensation'.[45]

The ideal state will require the right type of situation and territory which, again, are to be determined by its general aims.[46] The *polis* should aim to be self-sufficient and the ideal *polis* will therefore be established on land which can itself provide all, or nearly all, the required resources and materials. Very rich land, however, should be avoided to prevent the citizens from living in luxury. Security is also an important factor in choosing a site. Though the city will itself not wish to invade

---

[41] VII.7.i; ix (1327 b 20; 1328 a 18) 269; 270. [42] VII.16.

[43] II.6.x–xiii (1265 a 38–b 16) 70.   [44] II.7.v (1266 b 8–14) 73–4.

[45] VII.16.xv (1335 b 22–5) 294.   [46] VII.5.

any other state, it will not be able to ignore the danger of external attack. Aristotle thus does not carry idealism as far as planning for a world of peaceful states. The ideal state is imagined as existing among non-ideal and potentially hostile neighbours and must therefore be built in territory which is difficult to attack.[47]

How close should the city be to the sea? Aristotle discusses this question at slightly greater length[48] because he disagrees with Plato. Plato had argued in the *Laws* that the ideal state should not be a maritime state but should be at least 10 miles from the sea (a distance which because of the difficulties of land transport was quite considerable in ancient Greece). Plato's argument was based on what he thought had gone wrong with Athens. First, if a city was by the sea it would be visited by many foreigners, especially foreign traders, who would import new and corrupting ideas which would undermine the citizen's respect for tradition and authority. Secondly, a maritime state is likely to require a large navy. A large navy implies a large number of poor citizens to man the ships, a 'nautical mob', who will come to wield excessive power in the internal politics of the city. By contrast, a land-locked city will depend on its infantry, traditionally in Greece made up of citizens of moderate wealth.

Aristotle sympathizes with the need to prevent foreign contamination of the state's way of life and to avoid giving excessive power to the poor. But he also sees certain advantages in being close to the sea. A state will be more secure if it can defend itself and be supported by its allies on both land and sea. The ideal state will also need to engage in a certain amount of trade, importing materials and commodities it cannot itself produce and exporting its own surplus. Thus, though the state should be as self-sufficient as possible, Aristotle seems to believe that it cannot be completely self-sufficient. If it needs to trade, then it should have ready access to the sea. Characteristically he strikes a balance. By once again referring to the purpose of the state, he argues that it is possible to be close to the sea without necessarily encouraging the dangers envisaged by Plato. If the state is aiming at the good life and not at acquiring and maintaining an empire, it will not need a large fleet or a large body of sailors. Furthermore, what sailors there are can be excluded from the citizen body and placed under the command of soldiers. Similarly, if the state merely conducts its own trade and does not become a trading centre for other states it need not fear contamination from foreigners on a scale that cannot be controlled by law.

[47] Cf. II.6.vii–viii (1265 ^{a} 18–28) 69.   [48] VII.6.

Having indicated the principles which govern the choice of the right materials, Aristotle next considers how the legislator should use these materials. He gives a list, which is brief and incomplete, of the necessary elements which must exist in the ideal state. There must be food, crafts, arms, revenue, religion, adjudication of what is advantageous and just in men's dealings with one another.[49] This provides six necessary occupations or functions: farmers, craftsmen, fighting men, men of wealth, priests, and judges[50] to which labourers are later added.[51] He asks whether all inhabitants of the state should perform all functions or whether there should be separate groups for each, or at least for some, of them. As we would expect, the question is to be answered by reference to the purpose of the state. If the purpose of the state is that its members should lead the good life, then they must perform only those functions which are conducive to virtue and happiness. On this ground, Aristotle rules out commercial and unskilled work as demeaning and hostile to virtue and farming because it does not provide sufficient leisure for the life of virtue.[52] These occupations are to be left to people who, because they do not share in the end of the state, will not be full members of it but merely necessary conditions for its existence. Again we notice Aristotle's special contempt for urban occupations, for trade and manufacture, which foster values opposed to those of true virtue. Farm work, on the other hand, is not so corrupting. The objection to it is merely that the ordinary farm-worker is too busy to develop the intellectual and cultural virtues. Agriculture is an activity in which the gentleman may be interested, provided that he does not need to spend too much time in actual agricultural labour. However, as Aristotle had argued in Book One, even a leisurely interest in trade or manufacturing may be damaging. As in the aristocratic traditions of later Europe, it is quite acceptable to be a 'gentleman farmer', but the notions of 'gentleman retailer' or 'gentleman manufacturer' are suspect and paradoxical.

The functions which are to be reserved for the full members of the state are fighting, adjudication, which is expanded to include deliberation,[53] and religion. Deliberation and adjudication are the essential functions of citizenship and therefore must belong to the true members of the state. Aristotle does not mention the third element of govern-

[49] VII.8.vi–vii (1328 ^{b} 4–15) 272.   [50] VII.8.ix (1328 ^{b} 20–3) 272.
[51] VII.9.x (1329 ^{a} 36) 274.
[52] VII.9.iii–iv (1328 ^{b} 39–1329 ^{a} 2) 273; cf. VIII.2.iii–v (1337 ^{b} 5–21) 300–1.
[53] VII.9.iv (1329 ^{a} 3–4) 273.

ment, the official function (another instance of the cursory nature of his account of the ideal state), but presumably all magistrates and officials will also be drawn from the citizen class. Restricting priesthoods to the citizen class is in keeping with the Greek view that control of the state religion was one of the essential activities of government. Inclusion of the military function is justified more on practical than theoretical grounds. Because those who possess arms are able to 'decide whether the constitution is to continue or not',[54] it would be dangerous to leave military power in the hands of those who were not citizens. Though these three functions, political, religious, and military, should all be exercised by citizens, no citizen should perform them all at once. Fighting requires the strength of youth whereas political decision-making requires the experience and wisdom of maturity.[55] Religious duties can be conveniently left to the elderly in retirement.[56]

The sharp division of the citizen body into the young who fight and the mature who deliberate and govern raises difficulties. It is inconsistent both with Aristotle's account of citizenship and with his description of the ideal state as a species of political rule. Citizens have been defined as those who share in deliberative or judicial office but in the ideal state, it seems, there will be a large number of citizens who do not. Aristotle argues that the young will not mind.

No one really objects to this method of command by seniority or thinks himself too good for it; after all he knows that once he reaches the required age, he will get what he has earned by waiting.[57]

But this does not remove the theoretical difficulty. Though the young may not themselves resent their temporary exclusion from power, it is still true that they are counted as full members of the community and yet are not allowed to exercise the political rights of citizenship. Similarly, the government of the ideal state is meant to be a species of political rule where the citizens are at least proportionately equal and share in ruling and being ruled.[58] It is not easy to reconcile the requirement that a man will be a citizen for a considerable period of time before he is entitled to take his turn at ruling with the equality and alternation implied by political rule. Aristotle claims that in political rule the rulers learn to rule by being ruled[59] and counts the transition from being ruled to ruling which the citizen of the ideal state will pass

---

[54]   VII.9.v (1329 a 11–12) 274.   [55]   VII.9.vi (1329 a 14–16) 274.
[56]   VII.9.ix (1329 a 31–4) 274.   [57]   VII.14.v (1332 b 38–41) 286.
[58]   VII.14.iii (1332 b 25–9) 285.
[59]   VII.14.viii (1333 a 11–13) 286; cf. III.4.xiv (1277 b 8–13) 109–10.

through as an instance of alternation of ruling and being ruled. But it is an odd type of alternation because the young are not being treated as equals, even proportionately. Strictly speaking, the real political equals are the older citizens, the men who will together form the deliberative and judicial body and who will alternate the official functions among themselves. These are the only people who, on Aristotle's definition of citizenship, should really have been considered citizens and full members of the state. Indeed, he does sometimes distinguish between 'those of military age and those who share in the constitution' as if only the latter were citizens.[60] But, on the whole, he seems unwilling to circumscribe the citizen body so narrowly. It would be difficult to deny citizenship to the young adult sons of the ruling class who form the army and defend the state. They seem to be in a different category from those who are merely 'necessary conditions'; they are not engaged in menial labour but are being trained to take their place among the rulers. As members of the militia they are performing a function especially associated with citizenship in Greece. However, by not allowing them any share in decision-making, Aristotle has created a sharp division within a citizen body of supposed equals and has failed to reconcile his definition of citizenship with his view of who should hold power in the ideal state.

The final necessary element in the state is wealth. The total amount of wealth should be limited by the natural needs of the community.[61] Some of the land will be publicly owned and its produce will be used to provide revenue for public institutions, including the *syssitia* or communal dinners. *Syssitia* were formed by groups of citizens who met to eat together and their function was to encourage in peace time the collective solidarity and *esprit de corps* found among soldiers on campaign. They were found in Sparta, in certain Cretan cities, and in Carthage, that is in all the states Aristotle mentions in Book Two as having reputations for good government. He recommends them for his ideal state,[62] and though he does not give his reasons (he promises to do so later,[63] one of the many unfulfilled promises in Books Seven and Eight), it was, no doubt, their tendency to increase the unity and conformity of the citizen body which made them attractive to him. Most property will be privately owned, belonging to the citizen class who need wealth to provide the leisure necessary for the good life.[64] As

---

[60] VII.10.ix (1329 b 36–7) 276; VII.13.ix (1332 a 34–5) 284.
[61] Cf. VII.5.i–ii (1326 b 26–39) 266–77.   [62] VII.10.
[63] VII.10.x (1330 a 4–5) 276.
[64] VII.9.vi–viii (1329 a 17–26) 274.

we have seen, Aristotle opposes Plato's proposal in the *Republic* to abolish private property altogether for the ruling class. In general, he disagrees with those who think that private property is the cause of all or most conflict; a more important cause is the wickedness of human nature which must be improved by education and moral regulation.[65] For similar reasons, he opposes the suggestion of Phaleas that the political ills of the state would be cured by dividing private property equally between the citizens.[66] Phaleas considered equality in land only, whereas he should also have considered equality in slaves, stock, and money; equalizing property is useless unless one also limits population; it leaves undecided the question of the precise amount of property everyone should have; men are driven to political conflict for reasons other than a desire to have more than others; men are ambitious not only for wealth but for power. In general, men's desires are naturally insatiable and need to be controlled by education.

Aristotle's attack on this radical proposal for reorganizing the system of property reveals a zest, incisiveness, and attention to detail which suggest that he was much happier criticizing other people's ideal states than describing his own. His arguments also illustrate his deep mistrust of simple solutions. The economic structure of society may be one cause of political unrest but it is not the only cause. People's attitudes and behaviour, in other words, cannot be explained in purely economic terms. However, in spite of their trenchant common sense, these arguments ultimately lack conviction. Even if an alteration of the distribution of property is not the sole answer to society's ills, this does not prove that it is not part of the answer. Aristotle actually admits that equalization of property could do something, if not very much, to prevent social and political conflict, but he does not recommend such a policy for his ideal state. He accepts that there will be differing degrees of wealth among the citizen body and that some of the citizens of the ideal state may not be very well off. The reason why he does not adopt such a radical proposal we may suspect is simply that it is radical. Inequality of wealth was such an established feature of Greek society that, given Aristotle's respect for accepted values and institutions, its abolition must be unnatural and unjustifiable.

Aristotle also comments on the layout and planning of the city.[67] He is impressed by the aesthetic attractiveness of ordered town planning in which streets are laid out in a rectangular pattern. On the other hand,

---

[65] II.5.xi–xii (1263 ᵇ 15–27) 64–5.
[66] II.7.   [67] VII.11.

the old, haphazard type of layout provides better security in case of attack. Again, a compromise is to be sought: planned irregularity which can be both attractive and secure. He criticizes Plato's view that the ideal state should have no walls or fortifications. Plato, as often, had followed the example of the Spartans. Sparta was not fortified by defensive walls in the normal Greek fashion and the Spartans liked to claim that their city was defended not by stones but by the virtue of its citizens. Similarly, Plato had argued in the *Laws* that the citizens would grow soft if they relied on walls for their defence. Aristotle castigates this attitude as old-fashioned and attacks it in a series of typically forceful arguments:[68] cities which boasted in this way had in fact been destroyed; though it may be cowardly to shelter behind walls from an enemy of similar character and numbers, it is only prudent to do so when the enemy is superior in force; to refuse to have walls is like deliberately choosing a site which is easy to attack or like living in a house without walls for fear of becoming cowardly; those that have walls can choose whether to rely on them or not whereas those who have none have no such choice. The substance of this controversy may no longer be relevant but Aristotle's approach to it remains fresh. He again seems more at home in attacking than in constructing ideal states and shows the cast of his mind to be essentially anti-utopian.

Another interesting suggestion about the physical layout of the ideal state is the plan for more than one *agora*.[69] The *agora* in Greek cities was a central meeting-place, a market-place or city square, used for a variety of commercial, political, and social purposes. Aristotle, as we have seen, disapproves of commercial activity and especially of the buying and selling that took place in the *agora*. Though he does not intend to banish trade altogether from the ideal state, he believes that commercial activity is incompatible with true virtue. He has already stipulated that commerce and trade are to be conducted not by the citizens but by the 'necessary conditions', but he also wants to prevent the citizens from being contaminated by contact with traders. He therefore recommends two separate meeting-places, one for citizens only and another for traders.

Aristotle's account of the ideal state finishes with his incomplete treatment of education. It should be remembered that for Aristotle education and politics are closely related not separate activities. Politics has over-all responsibility for the achievement of human good while

---

[68] VII.11.viii–xii (1330 ^{b} 32–1331 ^{a} 18) 279–80.
[69] VII.12.

education is the most influential means towards this end. One must have the best materials and territory and also the right political and social institutions, but unless the education system is properly planned there will be little chance of establishing an ideal state. Hence the provision of education must be a matter of public concern. In most Greek cities education was not publicly provided or even publicly regulated but was left entirely to the initiative of individual families. In contrast to our own experience, it was writers of more conservative political views who showed most interest in, and support for, public education, because of the historical accident that education was publicly controlled only in conservative states like Sparta. But the principle that the state should direct the education of its young in accordance with its ideals is not necessarily either a conservative or a 'progressive' principle, as Aristotle himself recognizes.

Education must be related to the particular constitution in each case, for the character of the constitution is just that which makes it specifically what it is. Its own character made it at the start and continues to maintain it, the democratic character preserves democracy, the oligarchic an oligarchy.[70]

Once it is recognized that a constitution is more than just a set of lifeless laws and institutions and involves purposive behaviour by individuals and groups, the importance of education to the working of the constitution is obvious. If educational policy is not decided with reference to the particular type of government and social structure existing in the community, much social and political discord will follow. Though we may not accept some of the ethical and psychological assumptions of Aristotle's educational theory we must agree with the view, relatively rare in his time, that education is of great political importance.

Education in the ideal state will be directed towards realizing the goals of the ideal state, especially the achievement of the good life by the full members of the state. It is an aspect of the general control which the laws and the rulers will exercise over individual behaviour and is based on the same assumptions and principles that govern Aristotle's attitude to the role of law. There are three factors involved in education; nature, habit, and reason,[71] of which he discusses only the first two. The need for the appropriate natural qualities has already been discussed in the sections on the superiority of the Greek race and

[70] VIII.1.ii (1337 a 14–17) 299;cf. I.13.xv (1260 b 13–20) 53–4; V.9.xi–xiii (1310 a 12–22) 215–16.
[71] VII.13.xi (1332 a 39–40) 284; *EN* X.9 (1179 b 20–1).

on the regulation of marriage and childbirth. The emphasis on habit follows from Aristotle's view of morality and moral development. Only if people are first habituated to virtuous action will they become fully virtuous and choose right actions for the right reasons. In order to develop the right habits the young must be constantly supervised. They must be sheltered from bad influences, such as contact with people of inferior natures and character, bad language, stories, plays, and even music which may have a tendency to corrupt. Such censorship will be particularly strict with children but there is no doubt that Aristotle would like to see it continued for adults as well. He would have seen no value in allowing people the freedom to choose what is wrong; far better to compel them to do what is right in the hope that they will eventually learn to do it for its own sake. Several reasons for Aristotle's authoritarianism have already been suggested. Of particular importance for his educational theory is his view of political and ethical ideals as essentially static and unchanging. Though he recognizes that there has been some development up to his own age, he does not envisage any future change or development in human needs or values in later ages. This affects his approach to education. Provided that the older generation is educated in the correct moral and political values, education is simply a question of effectively passing these principles and values on to succeeding generations. Modern educational theory, by contrast, is based on the assumption that society is constantly changing. The younger generation therefore needs to be educated to deal with social problems which are at present unforseeable. Aristotle's assumption about the constancy of moral experience is not, it should be noted, confined to the ideal state where we might expect that by definition all change would be for the worse and must therefore be avoided. The same will apply in the imperfect states; the situations which await the younger generation in an oligarchy or a democracy are of the same type as those which formed the experience of the older generation. Just as there will be no need for continuing change in the laws, so there will be no need for sons to alter the principles and values of their fathers. Aristotle's authoritarianism in education thus depends in parts on a static or conservative view of society.

Additional note: The relation of the ideal state of Books Seven and Eight to Aristotle's account of aristocracy

In this chapter it has been assumed that the ideal state described in Books Seven and Eight is to be identified with Aristotle's true or ideal aristocracy. This assumption, however, is by no means undisputed and the reader should at least be aware of the main problems and the general reasons which support the present interpretation.

At the beginning of Book Four Aristotle says that kingship and aristocracy are the two forms of the best state where all power is in the hands of the virtuous.[72] In Book Three he describes the type of population suited to aristocracy as a people which 'can be governed by free persons who are in themselves leaders, as having the ability and virtue that are required for political rule.'[73] The ideal state of Books Seven and Eight fits these requirements. It is ruled by men of complete virtue and is said to be a species of political rule. The two main differences which have been said to exist between the ideal state and the earlier descriptions of aristocracy are not as sharp as has sometimes been thought. First, it is claimed that in Book Three Aristotle does not believe that more than a few men will ever be fully virtuous[74] whereas in Book Seven he seems more confident of finding a large number of virtuous people; in the ideal state the whole of the citizen body is fully virtuous.[75] But he may be referring here only to the ruling section of the citizen body. Even if he means to include the younger military element, this does not necessarily imply that a large number of men are virtuous. The size of the citizen body varies with the constitution and it is clear from the number of functions left to the 'necessary conditions' that the citizens will be an exclusive élite. Secondly, it has been argued that in the aristocracy of Book Three the division between rulers and ruled is regarded as permanent whereas in Book Seven the subjects, after a period of military service, become themselves qualified to rule. But this is not a crucial difference. As early as Book Three, Chapter Four, Aristotle says that, in the ideal state where rule is political, knowledge of ruling is acquired by the experience of being ruled.[76] Though usually he describes aristocracy as having a sharp division between rulers and ruled there is no suggestion that this is permanent or that the possibility of transition from one class to another is excluded. Indeed, the aristocracy in Book Three and the ideal state are similar in that both have political rule but do not alternate ruling and being ruled except in so far as the rulers learn by being ruled. If there is a contradiction, it is more within the account of the ideal aristocracy itself than between different accounts in different books.

[72] IV.2.i (1289 ^{a} 30–33) 151.   [73] III.17.iv (1288 ^{a} 9–11) 146.
[74] Cf. III.7.iv (1279 ^{a} 39–^{b} 2) 116.   [75] VII.13.ix (1332 ^{a} 32–5) 284.
[76] III.4.xiv (1277 ^{b} 8–13) 109–10.

CHAPTER SIX

PRACTICABLE PREFERENCES

Because few legislators, if any, will be in a position to establish an ideal state, political science, if it is to be of practical use, must also deal with non-ideal situations, with societies divided into groups of imperfect men whose interests conflict. This interest in everyday politics is one of Aristotle's most important innovations in political science and forms the basis for the so-called 'realistic' books of the *Politics*, Books Four to Six. In them he considers three main topics or groups of questions. The first, which we have already discussed, concerns the number of different types of constitution; the second, to be dealt with in this chapter, concerns the relative merits of non-ideal constitutions; the third, about the causes and prevention of political instability, will be discussed in the next chapter.

The Polity

The constitution which is best for most cities and most men is the polity. It is inferior to the ideal constitutions of true kingship and aristocracy though still superior to the three perverted forms of constitution—oligarchy, democracy, and tyranny.[1] Initially, polity is the good form of democracy but it later becomes a mixture of, or compromise between, oligarchy and democracy and it is its intermediate ·or moderate status which provides the reasons for its relative value. In the world of ordinary politics, the choice is between moderate or mixed constitutions, which are preferable, and pure, unadulterated constitutions, which are all inferior. The polity is not the only type of mixed constitution mentioned by Aristotle. There is also so-called aristocracy which differs from the polity by giving weight to the principle of merit or virtue as well as the principles of wealth and freedom. This difference, together with Aristotle's statement in criticism of Plato that the more constitutions are included as ingredients the better the mixture,[2] might lead us to expect that pride of place would be given to so-called aristocracy in Aristotle's account of the relatively best constitution. However, though so-called aristocracy might have a claim to be superior to the

---

[1] IV.8.i (1293 b 22–7) 165–6; IV.11.i (1295 a 25–31) 171.
[2] II.6.xviii (1266 a 4–5) 72.

polity, Aristotle does not accept it as a candidate for the best constitution for most cities and men. It either lies beyond the reach of most states or else is very close in nature to the polity and need not be discussed separately from the polity.[3] Another reason for ignoring so-called aristocracy, which Aristotle does not mention explicitly, is that it upsets the theoretical symmetry and elegance of his account. Given that oligarchy and democracy are the commonest forms of constitution, an assumption which runs through the central books of the *Politics*, it is logically simpler and more satisfying to concentrate on the constitution which is a mixture of these two forms alone.

Aristotle has several reasons for believing in the relative value of the mixed or moderate constitution. As we have seen, his discussion of equality and distributive justice in Book Three[4] provides a justification for such a constitution. Both the oligarch and the democrat are criticized for ignoring all claims except those of wealth and freedom respectively. By referring to the purpose of the state, Aristotle argues that honour and power should be distributed in accordance with both wealth and freedom as well as virtue. In a non-ideal state, where these qualities are possessed not by one group, but by different, though overlapping, groups, distributive justice will demand that all groups have a share in the constitution. Aristotle also describes two arguments for democracy which seem 'to contain some difficulty and perhaps some truth'.[5] In his opinion they justify not the complete sovereignty of the many, but rather the right of the many to a share in the constitution and they therefore support a mixed constitution which contains some democratic elements but is not completely democratic. These arguments are of particular interest for democratic theory and worth examining in some detail. The first may be called the argument of 'collective wisdom'.[6] A large body of men who are inferior as separate individuals may collectively be superior because each individual contributes his own share of virtue and practical wisdom to the group. When these contributions are added up, the group will be found to possess a greater sum of virtue and wisdom than a smaller number of individually wiser and more virtuous individuals. As with Aristotle's other 'mathematical' doctrines in ethics and politics, for example his theory of distributive justice in terms of proportion, we should not press the quantitative implications too far. He recognizes that ethics and politics are not capable of the same degree of precision as mathematics and is unlikely to have considered

[3] IV.11.ii (1295 a 31–4) 171.   [4] III.9; 12.
[5] III.11.i (1281 a 41–2) 122–3.   [6] III.11.ii–ix (1281 a 42–b 38) 123–4.

that the merits of individuals or groups can be mathematically calculated and compared. The addition is a metaphorical, not a literal, sum, a way of illustrating the belief, as we say, that 'two heads are better than one.'

Aristotle's belief in collective wisdom fits with his general respect for public opinion. But he does not claim that the many are invariably superior, only that they may be sometimes superior. Moreover, the collective superiority of the many, when it exists, will not give them a right to monopolize the functions of government. Magistracies, for example, must be held by a small number of individuals and here the many cannot exercise their superiority. The argument justifies the limited participation of the many in functions such as deliberation and adjudication and therefore provides support for the mixed constitution, which Aristotle, on this occasion, particularly associates with the Athenian lawgiver, Solon.

It was to avoid this that Solon and some of the other lawgivers gave to the people power to elect officers of government and to demand an account from them at the end of their tenure, but no right individually to hold such offices. This was in accord with our principle that the whole body of citizens acting together have the necessary understanding, even though each is individually not qualified to decide. By thus co-operating with the better sort of citizen the people can render some good service in their cities, in something like the same way that a combination of coarse foods with refined renders the whole diet more nutritious as well as more bulky.[7]

To justify the collective wisdom of the many, Aristotle begins with the analogy of the feast to which many contribute. This will be a better feast than one provided by a single individual, even if the many are individually poorer and their contributions inferior to that of a single individual. The quality of the feast is assumed to consist of a certain quantity of consumable objects such as food and drink and we can readily see how this can be made up of a large number of small individual contributions. This analogy may illustrate but it does not prove the collective superiority of the many, because there does not seem to be any similarly simple way of aggregating the individual contributions of virtue and wisdom. Aristotle also uses the analogy of aesthetic judgement.

The general public is a better judge of works of music and poetry; some judge some parts, some others, but their joint pronouncement is a verdict upon the whole.[8]

[7] III.11.viii–ix (1281 ^{b} 32–8) 124.
[8] III.11.iii (1281 ^{b} 7–10) 123.

Admittedly, different individuals may understand and appreciate different parts of a work of art but it does not follow from this that as a group they understand and appreciate the whole. Assuming that each of the individuals misunderstands at least part of the work it makes equally good sense to say that the group misunderstands the whole. One cannot establish that the collective judgement of the group is superior without specifying some way in which the good qualities of each individual coalesce into a collective judgement while the bad qualities are rejected. This Aristotle fails to do. He has been understood to mean that the superior collective judgement emerges through a process of public discussion and to be foreshadowing the modern view that democracy is a process of government by discussion. But he simply says that the people 'come together',[9] a vague description which would cover any sort of assembly or aggregation.

Aristotle adds another argument which is more convincing. According to Socrates and Plato, ruling was a skill like medicine or navigation, which implied that government, like these other skills, was a matter for properly trained and educated experts. Furthermore, just as the work of a doctor can only be properly assessed by other doctors, so in politics only the expert in the statesman's art can properly appoint or judge statesmen. Aristotle mentions this argument as a possible objection to the previous argument that the collective wisdom of the many may entitle them to a share in the deliberative or judicial functions and, in particular, to elect magistrates and call them to account. He meets the objection by saying that in some arts and skills the expert is not necessarily the best judge.

There are tasks of which the actual doer is not either the best or the only judge, cases in which even those who do not possess the operative skill pronounce an opinion on the finished product. An obvious example is house-building; the builder certainly can judge a house, but the user, owner or tenant, will be a better judge. So too the user of a rudder, the helmsman, is a better judge of it than the carpenter who made it; and it is the diner not the cook that pronounces upon the merits of the dinner.[10]

This argument concedes that the expert has specialized knowledge and skills, but refuses him the right to be above criticism or control. In the political sphere it means that those who are actually making decisions and carrying out the business of government should have specialized capacities and training but are not therefore exempt from lay control.

[9] III.11.ii; xiv (1281 ^{b} 5; 1282 ^{a} 17) 123; 125.
[10] III.11.xiv (1282 ^{a} 17–23) 125.

Though they alone may have the ability to devise and administer policy, they are not the ultimate judges of whether these policies are the right ones. It is the individual citizen who feels the effect of government action who can provide the final judgement on its merits. Like the argument of collective wisdom, this argument justifies a mixture of democracy and some more restrictive and élitist type of government. It is, however, a much better argument. The collective wisdom argument assumes that political decisions are like assessments of works of art which Aristotle saw as empirical judgements about independent matters of fact. On this view, it is difficult to argue that the population as a whole are likely to have opinions superior to those of the expert few. On the other hand, if political decisions are seen as decisions which affect the population and if the individual is assumed to be the best judge of how he ought to be affected, then the case for democratic rather than expert government is much stronger. Aristotle seems to hesitate about accepting this argument, perhaps because in the ideal state it is the rulers not the subjects who know best. But even if his support is partial and hesitant, he has at least recognized and understood an argument which can be used to rebut the more authoritarian implications of the view that politics is a skill.

So far the arguments supporting the polity have been arguments for a constitution which favours both democratic and oligarchic principles and combines both democratic and oligarchic institutions. In Book Four, however, the arguments depend more on the social composition of the polity and from this point of view the polity is more a moderate than a mixed constitution. In institutional structure it may be a mixture of oligarchic and democratic principles and institutions but socially it is not a mixture or balance between rich and poor but a constitution in which the middle class dominate. In Book Four, therefore, Aristotle argues for the relative superiority of the polity in terms of the superiority of the middle class over the rich and the poor and not in terms of the superiority of a mixture of democracy and oligarchy over either of these constitutions in an unmixed form.[11] Aristotle's middle class is defined with reference to the amount of their property. When talking of 'the middle class', we should remember that Aristotle's term is 'those in the middle' (*hoi mesoi*) and we must not import any modern, Marxist connotations of the *bourgeoisie* or of a specific relation to the means of production. 'Those in the middle' are simply those of moderate or

[11] IV.11.

medium wealth. They are the men who could afford the armour of the hoplite or heavy-armed infantryman and thus formed the core of the city's military power on land.

Aristotle gives a number of arguments, of varying cogency, in favour of the superiority of the middle class. First, he draws an analogy with the doctrine of the mean from the *Ethics.*

If we were right when in our Ethics we stated that Virtue is a Mean and that the happy life is life free and unhindered and according to virtue, then the best life must be the middle way, consisting in a mean between two extremes which it is possible for each individual to attain. And the same principle must be applicable to the goodness or badness of states and constitutions.[12]

This illustrates Aristotle's general preference for moderation and the middle way in ethics and politics but it does not prove that the rule of the middle class is best. The doctrine of the mean in the *Ethics* is concerned with the individual's disposition to act. The character of the ethically virtuous man is such that he has his emotions in balance and does not act or even wish to act with extremes of pity, fear, amusement, and so on. For example, the courageous man avoids the twin extremes of rashness and cowardice. But even if we accept this doctrine as an analysis of ethical action, Aristotle's use of it to prove the superiority of the middle class is invalid. If we draw a parallel between the life of the individual and the life of the state, we should say that the state ought to act in a moderate way. It should not, for example, be too adventurous or too cautious in its policies. But this does not prove that the constitution should be in the hands of the middle class. To prove this we need another premiss, that the men of moderate means are most likely to act together moderately. This premiss requires further proof and thus the bare argument from analogy is not in itself sufficient.

Secondly, Aristotle claims that those who have a moderate amount of gifts of fortune, including wealth, are more likely to 'follow reason'.[13] The wealthy are inclined to insolence and great crimes and the poor to roguery and petty crimes. As insolence and roguery are the two sources of crime, the middle class are most likely to be law-abiding and therefore reasonable. It might be objected that, if the rich tend to commit great crimes and the poor petty crimes, then the middle class will commit middling crimes which would not make them especially reasonable and law-abiding. But Aristotle may intend this argument not as a logical

[12] IV.11.iii (1295 a 35–40) 171.
[13] IV.11.iv–v (1295 b 1–11) 171–2.

proof but as a statement of sociological fact; extremes of wealth or poverty are likely to prevent the development of virtue. Admittedly, he does not believe that moderate wealth is a sufficient condition or guarantee of virtue. As he said in criticism of Phaleas, it is not enough to ensure a moderate amount of property for the citizens; one must educate them to obey the laws.[14] But he certainly believes that poverty is a bar to virtue and reasonableness and that great wealth is unnecessary and unnatural. In their level of material prosperity, if not in their moral development, the middle class match the citizens of the ideal state.

The other arguments in favour of the middle class point to their more specifically political qualities. A city in which the middle class dominate is more likely to have 'free' government and is also most likely to incorporate friendship and equality:

Those who have a super-abundance of all that makes for success, strength, riches, friends, and so forth, neither wish to be ruled nor understand how to be; and this is ingrained in them from childhood on; even at school they are so full of their superiority that they have never learned to do what they are told. Those on the other hand who are greatly deficient in these qualities are too subservient. So they cannot command and can only obey in a servile regime, while the others cannot obey in any regime and can command only in a master-slave relationship. The results is a state not of free men but of slaves and masters, the one full of envy, the other of contempt. Nothing could be farther removed from friendship or from the whole idea of a shared partnership in a state. Sharing is a token of friendship; one does not share even a journey with people one does not like. The state aims to consist as far as possible of those who are like and equal, a condition found chiefly among the middle section. And so the best government is certain to be found in this kind of city, whose composition is, we maintain, a natural one.[15]

The argument of this section is important and requires careful analysis. It may be summarized as follows: the rich are unaccustomed to being ruled but accustomed to ruling despotically; the poor are unaccustomed to ruling but accustomed to being ruled despotically; the rich and the poor will therefore together form a city of masters and slaves not of free men; a city should have friendship and equality which come most from the middle class; therefore the rule of the middle class is best. We may perhaps agree that the rich are unlikely to accept the rule of another, less wealthy, group and that their rule will tend to be selfish and therefore despotic. But the second point is more dubious. Is Aristotle right in thinking that the poor are unable to exercise rule and

[14] II.7.viii (1266 ^{b} 28–31) 74.
[15] IV.11.vi–viii (1295 ^{b} 13–28) 172.

are fit only for being ruled as slaves? Elsewhere in the *Politics* he does not see the poor in such a docile and servile light; as a group, they tend to aim for power and domination in a way similar to, rather than opposite from, the rich. In this passage he has assumed a false opposition between rich and poor in order to argue that the middle class occupy a middle and mean position: they neither rule despotically nor obey slavishly but alternate between ruling and being ruled in a free and undespotic manner. He thus attempts to establish an intrinsic political superiority for the members of the middle class. But he does not convince. There is no reason why the rich or the poor should be any less willing than members of the middle class to share in ruling and being ruled with members of their own class. Nor is there any reason to believe that those who hold a moderate amount of wealth will be any more prepared to share their rule with members of a class whose interests are as diametrically opposed to their own as those of the rich are to those of the poor and *vice versa*. What is more likely to make the rule of the middle class less despotic and more equal is the fact that, given a division of society into rich, poor, and middle class, there is no class as opposed to the middle class as the rich and the poor are to one another. The middle class can be expected to treat the poor more leniently than the rich do and the rich more leniently than the poor do. But in this case, the superiority of the middle class, if it exists, is a product not of their intrinsic qualities but of their relative position in the social structure.

A similar criticism can be made of the argument that the middle-class constitution has more friendship and equality, two qualities which are essential to any proper *koinonia*. With reference to these principles, it makes sense to say that a citizen body divided into very rich and very poor will be deficient as a community. But again the argument depends on the relative not the intrinsic qualities of the classes. There will be no equality and friendship between rich and poor. It does not follow that there will be no equality and friendship between members of the same class, between rich men or between poor men. Yet this is what Aristotle implies. He says that friendship and equality exist especially among members of the middle class whereas he is entitled to say only that there will be more friendship and equality in a state where there is a large dominant middle class. The reason will be not that middle class people are intrinsically more given to equality or friendship but that in a community with a large middle class the economic and political divisions within the community are likely to be much less stark. In this section then, though Aristotle may have indicated some grounds for justifying the mediating role of the middle class, he has overstated the case in an attempt to prove its moral and political superiority.

Aristotle also argues that a state dominated by the middle class is more likely to achieve stability, a political goal which he values very highly, especially for ordinary, non-ideal states.[16] The middle class is the most secure and stable group in the community in that its members do not have enough wealth to be the object of envy or attack while they are sufficiently well off not to wish to attack the rich. The observation that the middle class is least likely to be a cause of economic grievance and conflict seems a reasonable one. It stems from the fact that the middle class in general is not opposed to either the rich or the poor to the same extent that the rich and the poor are opposed to one another. The existence of a strong middle class can therefore prevent the antagonism of the rich and the poor from causing strife and revolution. If either of these classes aims at revolution then the middle class can count on the support of the other class in quelling it.[17] The middle class thus acts as a buffer between the rich and the poor. It also provides the only hope of a government consented to by all the citizens. The rich and the poor will not consent to be ruled by one another but they are both likely to consent to be ruled by the middle class who play the role of arbiter or mediator.

But on all occasions the mediator is well trusted and the one in the middle is mediator.[18]

These arguments, which depend on the central, balancing role of the middle class, are theoretically plausible and appear to be confirmed by experience. Communities which are polarized into two groups of rich and poor do appear to be less stable politically than those in which there is a substantial middle class. Though a balance between opposing political principles may produce stability, as in the mixed constitution of Sparta, famous for its resistance to change, a balance between opposing classes without any middle class, will lead to instability.[19] Aristotle rightly recognizes the importance of economic divisions in political conflict and the need to reduce and blur these divisions in order to achieve political harmony and stability. Though he sometimes

[16] IV.11.ix (1295 ^{b} 28–34) 172.
[17] Cf. IV.12.iv (1296 ^{b} 38–40) 175.
[18] IV.12.v (1297 ^{a} 5–6) 176.
[19] Cf. V.4.xi (1304 ^{a} 38–^{b} 2) 199.

overstates the virtues of the middle class, he is right to recognize its stabilizing influence in the community.

The polity provides a standard for judging the absolute merit of ordinary constitutions.[20] As we have seen, Aristotle's classification of the types of oligarchy and democracy involves a progression, in each case, from the most moderate to the most extreme. In both cases the moderate form borders on the polity. The polity is thus the standard from which oligarchies and democracies deviate and the further they deviate, the worse they become. The classification of democracy and oligarchy and their different species, like many of Aristotle's classifications, is designed to help evaluation as well as analysis. Though the polity is the best type of constitution for most cities, it has not existed often.[21] The middle class is usually small; when the rich or the poor establish a constitution after a revolution, they tend to pervert the constitution to their own interests as a prize for victory; states with powerful influence in Greece have not encouraged the adoption by other cities of this middle type of constitution; even if one could persuade influential groups and individuals to accept the value of the polity, the lack of a sufficiently large middle class in most states will necessarily prevent them from adopting the polity as their constitution. How then can the polity really be said to be the best for most cities if it is beyond the reach of most cities? The inconsistency is less real than it appears. Aristotle does not actually say that the polity is a constitution which most cities can achieve, only that it is the best, judging from the standard of a constitution which most cities can 'share' or 'have a part in'.[22] Many cities which cannot become full polities can at least have some of the characteristics of the polity and be said to have a share in it. The function of the polity is to provide a goal at which ordinary states, which are mostly oligarchies or democracies, can aim, even if they cannot reach it entirely. They should not, however, try to be closer to the polity than is appropriate for their particular community. When answering the question of what constitution is most suited for most cities,[23] Aristotle gives a general principle which should determine the choice of a constitution in any city:

that part of the state which desires the maintenance of the constitution should be stronger than that which does not.[24]

---

[20] IV.11.xx–xxi (1296 b 3–9) 174.
[21] IV.11.xvi–xix (1296 a 22–b 1) 173–4.
[22] IV.11.i (1295 a 31) 171.   [23] IV.12.
[24] IV.12.i (1296 b 15–16) 175.

With his awareness of the intimate connection between political institutions and the underlying social structure he recognizes that it is useless to impose a constitution on a society which cannot support it or make it work. Given the socio-economic structure of most Greek states, either democracy or oligarchy is likely to be the most appropriate form of constitution. But the legislator should make every attempt to temper the constitution by involving the middle class in it.[25] As far as their social composition will allow, all states should aim to possess at least some of the characteristics of the polity.

Aristotle's theory of the polity is different in several respects from later theories of the mixed constitution. Aristotle does not, like Polybius and Cicero, support a mixture of the three main types, rule of the one, of the few, and of the many, but of only two. Nor, like Montesquieu and the founders of the American constitution, does he argue for a balance between the different powers or functions of government, that is the legislature, the executive, and the judiciary. Institutionally the polity is a mixture of, or compromise between, the procedures and principles of different types of constitution. Again, Aristotle's theory is concerned not just with institutions but also with the social structure which supports them and which they serve. On this level it is less a theory of mixture than of moderation. The polity does not rest on a balance between rich and poor but on the dominance of the middle class. None the less, though the account of the polity is unique in many of its details, it is similar to subsequent theories of the mixed constitution in its assumption of the value of moderation and of the need to avoid political extremes. In general inspiration, then, it may be said to belong to the tradition of the mixed constitution.

Though Aristotle's account of the polity is open to certain objections, they should not be allowed to obscure the real and lasting value of this part of his political theory. Its importance has to some extent been masked by a shift in our political terminology. What many people today describe and defend as 'democracy' has more in common with Aristotle's polity than with his democracy. For instance, those who hold that there should be regular elections every few years but would not approve of annual elections or of submitting all major decisions to referenda are really subscribing to Aristotle's view that the best constitution in the non-ideal world is one which combines oligarchic and democratic procedures. Furthermore, research by political sociologists

[25] IV.12.iv (1296 ^{b} 34–8) 175.

has tended to confirm Aristotle's observation that stability is unlikely to be achieved in states where there is a sharp division into rich and poor. There is a much greater chance of avoiding dissidence and revolution when the government is in the hands of, or at least has the support of, a large middle class. More generally, Aristotle is to be commended for making a clear distinction between the ideal constitution and the constitution which may serve as a standard and model for ordinary constitutions. Great harm can and has been done by using utopian standards to judge ordinary situations and by trying to impose political institutions which may be suitable for an ideal situation, in which men have achieved their full moral and intellectual potential, on people and societies whose characters and needs are far from ideal. Aristotle takes great care to avoid this mistake. He distinguishes the ideally best from the practicable best and also points out that the practicable best, the polity, is not suited to all situations; there will be cases where it would be wrong to impose a polity rather than an oligarchy or a democracy. As so often, he shows too much respect for phenomena, in this case the needs and characters of ordinary states and their citizens, to wish to fit them into an inappropriate pattern, however, theoretically attractive it may seem.

The Deviant Constitutions

After the relative merits of the three 'normal' types of constitution, Aristotle's ranking of the three deviant constitutions, democracy, oligarchy, and tyranny, remains to be considered. Tyranny he considers to be the worst of the three, with oligarchy the second worst and democracy the best, or least bad. One reason for ranking them in this order is that the tyranny is the perversion of the best form, kingship, while oligarchy is the perversion of the next best, aristocracy.[26] In its logical and schematic approach this argument is similar to Plato's ranking of constitutions in the *Statesman*, though it differs in detail. But Aristotle has gone beyond such a simplistic method of classifying and evaluating constitutions and will therefore not be satisfied with a similar approach to their ranking. This argument for the especially evil nature of tyranny will not work because kingship is no longer clearly the best type of constitution. Moreover, some of the characteristics traditionally associated with tyranny, such as extreme self-interest and lawlessness, have also been attributed to extreme oligarchy and

[26] IV.2.ii (1289 a 39–b 5) 152; cf. *EN* VIII.10 (1160 a 35–b 21).

democracy. Tyranny cannot therefore be said to be worst simply because it possesses these characteristics. In Greek political theory, however, tyranny stood for the utter perversion of the principles of good government and so there could be little doubt that tyranny was the worst form of government, almost by definition. Aristotle's solution is to argue that tyranny is especially evil because it combines the particular evils of both oligarchy and democracy and attacks both the poor and the rich.[27] This is a good example of how he reconciles the claims of historical accuracy and of theoretical symmetry. The particular characteristics of tyranny are drawn from observation and accumulated historical experience, but he manages to fit them into his general classification of constitutions, thus preserving, in a revised and improved form, the traditional maxim that tyranny is the worst form of government.

Aristotle's preference for democracy over oligarchy is already suggested in Book Three where, after criticizing both types of government for having faulty conceptions of justice, he nevertheless concedes that the claims of the many may have some weight. In Book Four, using a musical metaphor, he says that oligarchy and democracy are both deviations from the 'harmony' or 'attunement' of the well-mixed constitution, but oligarchy is more 'taut and despotic' while democracy is more 'slack and soft'.[28] We catch a hint of Plato's argument in the *Statesman* that democracy is less effective than oligarchy and therefore has less power to do evil. But Aristotle does not pursue this argument. Instead, his main reason for preferring democracy is that it is more stable than oligarchy. Democracies tend to have larger middle classes and to give them a larger share in government than oligarchies do. They are therefore more stable because the middle class is the most stable class.[29] A further reason for the greater instability of oligarchy is that the ruling groups in oligarchies are more prone to internal dissension which threatens the general stability of the state.[30] Aristotle does not offer any evidence or reasons for the comparative solidarity of the poor but it accords with a general bias against oligarchy which he often displays by his tone and emphasis rather than by actual argument. His preference for democracy over oligarchy, however, applies in general terms only. It does not mean that any democracy is preferable to any oligarchy. Of much greater significance is the relative superiority and inferiority of different types of oligarchy and democracy, depending

[27] V.10.xi–xii (1311 ^{a} 8–20) 218.   [28] IV.3.viii (1290 ^{a} 27–9) 154.
[29] IV.11.xiv (1296 ^{a} 13–18) 173.   [30] V.1.xv–xvi (1302 ^{a} 8–13) 192.

on the extent to which they approximate to the polity at one end of the scale and to the extreme or pure type at the other. The more moderate type of oligarchy will usually be preferable to the more extreme type of democracy.

CHAPTER SEVEN

POLITICAL DISORDER

In Books Five and Six Aristotle deals with the last of the three topics announced at the beginning of Book Four, the protection of particular constitutions against constitutional change and disorder. These books have often been neglected because of a tendency to concentrate on Aristotle's political ideals and on the contrast between these ideals and those of Plato's *Republic.* Yet they contain much that is of more than historical interest not just in matters of substance but also in general method and approach. In several respects they come closest to Aristotle's view of political science as an intellectual discipline. In the first place, the method of exposition is more straightforward, especially in Book Five, than in most of the other books. There is less dialectical discussion of problems or of his predecessor's views. Instead, the evidence and conclusions are set out in a logical order, and criticism of Plato, for example, is postponed to what amounts to an appendix.[1] These books, however, are by no means completely finished. Both end abruptly as if they were meant to be continued. Even as they stand they are in need of further revision. For example, the account of the causes of constitutional change includes a number of afterthoughts or postscripts which should have been incorporated into earlier parts of the analysis. Moreover, certain causes of constitutional change mentioned elsewhere in the *Politics* are omitted altogether. None the less, though Aristotle would not have claimed that he was giving a final or definitive account of the topic, he has indicated the general form that political science should ultimately take.

Secondly, these books make most use of the research into the history and workings of individual constitutions which was carried out by Aristotle and his pupils. Political science, if it is a science, must deal with the general rather than the particular case but its generalizations must be based on empirical evidence; hence the need to organize research into individual constitutions. The empirical research was thus inspired by the demands of theory and both the questions asked and the answers discovered would have been influenced by theoretical preoccupations. Aristotle was not interested in facts for their own sake.

[1] V.12.

At the same time his preoccupations were themselves based on a deep acquaintance with Greek political life and we cannot say that theory is completely prior to fact. As with many scientists, the theoretical and the empirical constantly interact in a way that eludes simple analysis. In the use he makes of empirical evidence Aristotle illustrates his belief that mathematical precision is not possible in political science. By the frequent use of phrases such as 'especially' or 'for the most part' he reminds us that his generalizations are not meant to be universal but admit of possible or actual counter-examples.[2] Indeed, it might be argued that he is excessively imprecise, that he could have achieved a greater rigour in his causal analysis. When making a generalization he is usually content to quote one or two examples in its support. He shows no interest in expressing the degree of support in statistical terms as we would expect a modern social scientist to do. He does not say, for example, that a certain type of behaviour occurred in eleven out of seventeen observed cases. He seems to have been content to indicate the varying degrees of empirical support for his generalizations in qualitative rather than quantitative terms, by such words as 'usually', 'sometimes', or 'occasionally'.

The final respect in which these books illustrate Aristotle's view of political science is that the empirical discussion of political behaviour is clearly related to a practical purpose, the securing of political stability. The phenomena of political disorder and constitutional change are investigated not simply as objects of scientific interest but in order that the statesman may learn how to avoid them. The analysis of causes leads directly to the giving of advice to the statesman, just as the explanation of disease helps the doctor to administer the cure. Political science is thus clearly seen to be a practical science. This does not mean that Aristotle's causal analysis is necessarily value-laden or distorted by the practical aim. He recognizes that the two aspects of analysis and advice are conceptually distinct. Though his analysis may sometimes have been influenced by his political preferences, this is not an inevitable consequence of his use of his results for a practical purpose. Similar distortion may be found in the work of political scientists whose aims are purely academic. What the practical purpose determines is not the analysis of the phenomena but rather the choice of what phenomena to analyse. Political instability is chosen as a subject of study because it is bad and ought to be avoided. Thus, though Books Five and Six are

---

[2] e.g. V.1.i (1301 a 22, 24) 189; V.5.i; xi (1304 b 20–1; 1305 a 35) 200; 202.

rightly called the most 'scientific' or 'empirical' books of the *Politics,*
we must not forget that their ultimate purpose is moral and practical.

Constitutional Change and Stasis

Aristotle announces his subject at the beginning of Book Five as the
investigation of constitutional change.

We have still to discuss what are the causes of change in constitutions,
their nature and number, what are the destructive agencies that affect
each constitution, and from what kinds into what kinds they generally
change. We must likewise consider what factors make for the preservation of constitutions, both in general and of each kind separately, also by
what means each of the types of constitution could best be preserved.[3]

Almost immediately, however, the area of inquiry is broadened to
include the causes not only of constitutional change but also of *stasis.*[4]
Stasis is a term which cannot be satisfactorily translated into English. It
is used by Aristotle to refer to a certain type of political conflict within
a state. Not all internal conflict, however, counts as *stasis.* It is distinguished from the milder 'rivalry' or competition for office between
individuals and groups[5] and also from outright warfare.[6] A common
synonym for *stasis* is *tarache,* meaning 'disorder' or 'confusion' and, in
its political connotation, close to the Irish 'troubles'. Roughly speaking,
the essence of *stasis* is that it involves the attempt to seize power by
those who are prepared to use violence or other illegal means. The
difference between *stasis* and more legitimate forms of political competition is imprecise, partly because of a corresponding lack of clarity
in Greek notions of what is legal or illegal. Greek states used both
written and unwritten laws and, as a result of their political instability
and discontinuity, were often without clearly recognizable constitutional
conventions. The line dividing legitimate from illegitimate political conflict was therefore not clear and would often itself be a matter of
political contention between competing groups. Though most would
have agreed that *stasis* involved taking the struggle for power beyond
the limits of what was acceptable or lawful, there would often be disagreement about whether these limits had actually been crossed.

Though *stasis* and constitutional change usually go together, each
can occur without the other. First, *stasis* need not involve constitutional
change. It may be aimed simply at the gaining of power within the
existing constitutional framework or at a minor modification rather

---

[3] V.1.i (1301 ᵃ 20–5) 189.   [4] V.1.vi (1301 ᵃ 39) 190.
[5] V.3.ix (1303 ᵃ 14) 195.   [6] V.3.xiii (1303 ᵇ 1–2) 196.

than a full scale change in the constitution.[7] Secondly, constitutional change may óccur without *stasis*.[8] The change may be brought about peacefully by a deliberate decision on the part of the governing body to alter the rules determining their own composition and so alter the constitution itself. Alternatively, the constitution may change accidentally when no one has deliberately intended a change. For example, if there is a change in the general level of economic wealth in a community, a property qualification, though itself unaltered, may produce a change in the relative size of the governing body.[9] Because Aristotle includes this unintentional type of constitutional change, it is misleading to use the word 'revolution' as an equivalent for 'constitutional change'. 'Revolution' usually implies the use of violence or at least a conscious intent to change the constitution.

Thus the subject matter of Books Five and Six includes two separate phenomena, *stasis* and constitutional change. Because each can occur without the other, neither can be classed as a species or type of the other. Yet it was natural for Aristotle to treat them together. Both are types of what we may call general political 'instability' or 'disorder' which threaten the pursuit of Aristotle's good life and which he considers most rulers are anxious to avoid. Moreover, in most cases they do accompany one another; *stasis* usually leads to a constitutional change and constitutional change is usually brought about by *stasis*. These central cases which include both phenomena may properly be called 'revolutionary'. The fact that Aristotle does not restrict himself to this central core but also includes non-revolutionary constitutional change and non-revolutionary *stasis* might be thought to blur the focus of his investigation. Yet the modern study of revolution shows that great problems are caused by attempts to define the phenomenon too closely. This appears to be a case where Aristotle's lack of precision pays dividends. By not defining his terms too precisely, he is not forced arbitrarily to exclude evidence which is relevant to his central theme.

The General Causes of Disorder

In describing the causes of constitutional change and *stasis* Aristotle begins with those which apply generally to all constitutions before describing causes which are peculiar to individual types. This method fits with his view of the proper logical order for scientific knowledge. Though inquiry and investigation, the acquiring of scientific knowledge,

---

[7] V.1. viii–xi(1301 ^{b} 10–26) 190–1.   [8] V.3.ix–x (1303 ^{a} 13–25) 195.
[9] V.6.xvi–xvii (1306 ^{b} 6–16) 205; V.8.x–xi (1308 ^{a} 35–^{b} 10) 210–11.

may proceed from the particular to the general, science itself, in its finished state, proceeds in the reverse direction, beginning with the most general and fundamental principles of the discipline and then moving step by step to the less general and the more specific. In spite of important differences in the subject matter and the types of argument appropriate for particular scientific disciplines, this pattern holds good for all. Political disorder is analysed in three such stages. Aristotle begins with what applies to all constitutions, though he does not include all six types of constitution under this heading but makes a broad distinction between 'constitutions', covering oligarchy, democracy, polity, and aristocracy, and 'monarchies', that is kingship and tyranny. The next stage involves causes in the four main types of constitution, and later, in the two types of monarchy. This is as far as Aristotle goes in Book Five. In Book Six, however, a third stage of particularity is introduced in the discussion of separate sub-types, though the discussion is confined to the sub-types of democracy and oligarchy and is directed less to the reasons for instability than to the methods of preventing it.

Of causes applying generally to all constitutions the most important is differing conceptions of justice and equality. Aristotle's analysis of equality and distributive justice is by now familiar. At the beginning of Book Five[10] he repeats his distinction between arithmetic and geometric equality, that is between absolute and proportionate equality. Though all men agree in the abstract that justice is proportionate, that goods and political power should be distributed equally according to merit and desert, they disagree about the nature of such merit and desert. In particular, some people (democrats) consider that as they are equal in one respect (free birth) they should be equal in all, while others (oligarchs) think that as they are unequal in one respect (wealth) they should be unequal in all. Though other criteria such as noble birth and virtue are briefly mentioned,[11] Aristotle considers the conflict between the oligarchic and democratic principles of justice to be the most widespread and most important. Democracy and oligarchy were the two commonest forms of constitution in Greece and the opposition between them, as we have seen, is one of the underlying themes of the central books of the *Politics*. Differing conceptions of justice, which lead to differing criteria for the distribution of office and political power and hence to different constitutions, are the basic cause of *stasis* and constitutional change. When men are excluded from power and wish to

---

[10] V.1.
[11] V.1.vi–vii; xiv (1301 ^{a} 40–^{b} 4; 1301 ^{b} 40–1302 ^{a} 2) 190; 191.

seize it for themselves, they do so in the belief that the existing distribution of power is unjust. The injustice which leads to dissatisfaction and instability is at first described as if it were genuine injustice or injustice according to Aristotle's own standards.[12] But if this were a necessary condition for *stasis* and change, there could be no instability where power was justly distributed. This would be a somewhat naïve position which Aristotle does not adopt. He later makes it clear that a subjective feeling of injustice is sufficient as a cause of dissidence[13] though we may assume that such a feeling of injustice is more likely to be produced where actual injustice exists.

By making this cause the first and most fundamental Aristotle again moves from the more general to the more particular in the way that is proper for scientific knowledge. Distributive justice is part of the essential core not only of all constitutions but also of all social groups or *koinoniai*. By beginning his analysis of constitutional change and *stasis* with this concept, he is able to link the account of one particular aspect of political behaviour to its wider context in political theory as a whole. But his reasons are unlikely to be wholly formal or methodological. He also wishes to make an important, substantial point about dissident and revolutionary movements. Such individuals or groups usually act in pursuit of a general principle. Admittedly, they are seldom purely idealistic in the sense of having no thought for their own personal and material interests; as Aristotle constantly emphasizes, there is a close connection between a man's social and economic status within the community and his political principles, especially his conception of political justice. On the other hand, successful movements are rarely based on purely selfish motives without any concern for moral principles.[14] Aristotle would disagree with those political analysts who argue that the appeal to moral principle is merely hypocrisy, a front to gain support. By making the sense of injustice the fundamental cause he implies that the revolutionary is motivated by genuine feelings of injustice. This cause cannot apply to those instances of constitutional change which are accidental or unintended. But this is a minor exception which Aristotle would readily have admitted and which does not damage his account. He makes no claim to be speaking categorically or without exception and the looseness with which his subject matter is determined must produce a corresponding looseness in his generalizations.

He adds two further causes which apply in all cases. One is the end

---

[12] V.1.xi (1301 ᵇ 26–9) 191.
[13] V.2.ii–iii (1302 ᵃ 24–31) 192.   [14] Cf. V.12.xiv (1316 ᵃ 39–ᵇ 3) 234.

or goal of the dissidents.[15] Aristotle considers the object aimed at, or the final cause, to be an important part of the explanation of any movement, whether human, animal, or even inanimate. Though we may agree with philosophers of science who criticize him for including goals and purposes in his scientific explanations of physical phenomena, we may be more prepared to accept them in explanations of deliberate human action. If we wish to understand the revolutionary, we shall want to know the object he has in mind. Again, we shall not expect to find an aim in the cases where change is unintentional; where there is no intention there will be no purpose. The dissident's object is profit and honour or their opposites; men revolt either to acquire profit and honour, which includes political power, or to avoid being deprived of them. Profit and honour embrace two aspects of social life, the economic and the political. Modern political scientists sometimes argue about which of these two aims is to be given priority. Do men seek wealth in order to gain political power or political power in order to gain wealth? For Aristotle, both are desired for their own sake.

The third general cause is really a number of more specific causes. While the sense of injustice and the desire for profit and honour are common to all, or nearly all, instances of change and *stasis,* there are other causes which may affect any type of constitution, yet are not found in all or even in most instances. These causes are treated at much greater length and with frequent use of examples.[16] The first two are profit (1) and honour (2), which have already appeared in the second general cause, as the objects aimed at. As causes in the third group they are properties belonging to those in power who provoke rebellion by the fact that they possess honour and wealth and by the way they use them. The difference is a real one: men's desire for profit and honour may be intensified and activated by seeing their rulers possessing them. The next cause is *hybris* (3) usually translated as 'insolence' but in Greek a wider and stronger term, covering not only arrogance towards subordinates but also acts of violence and sexual violation and having strong overtones of contempt for religion. The fourth cause is pre-eminence, not simply the pre-eminence that any rulers must have but the excessive superiority when one or more individuals exercise power 'out of all proportion to the state or to the power of the citizen body'.[17] This sort of excess of power may lead to a monarchy or family oligarchy and justifies the institution of ostracism by which such people are

---

[15] V.2.iii (1302 a 31–4) 192–3.   [16] V.3.

[17] V.3.iii (1302 b 15–17) 193.

banished. The next two causes are fear (5) and contempt (6). Fear operates, for example, when men expect to be punished for some crime and aim to seize power in order to avoid punishment; or when they expect injury from those in power and seek to prevent it. Contempt refers not to the attitude of rulers to ruled, which is covered by *hybris,* but that of ruled to rulers when subjects despise those in power and therefore reject their claim to rule. The seventh cause is disproportionate increase (7) which Aristotle describes by means of a biological analogy. If a part of the body increases in size relatively to the other parts, the form and nature of the animal will change. Similarly, if one social class grows in relation to the other classes, the constitution will no longer fit the social composition of the state. The relative increase may be caused either by the actual growth or by the actual decrease of one class or section of the community. When it occurs the newly predominate class will agitate for change. This cause of *stasis* and constitutional change is similar to the fourth cause, pre-eminence. The difference between them is partly one of degree. Whereas pre-eminence refers to the relative superiority of an individual or small group of people, disproportionate increase refers to whole classes, especially the rich and the poor. Moreover, pre-eminence appears to be restricted to those already in power, whereas disproportionate increase is typically a growth in a class excluded from power.

To these seven causes Aristotle adds four more.[18] Three are causes which produce constitutional change without *stasis:* election contests (8), carelessness (9), when, for example, someone who is disloyal to the constitution is inadvertently appointed to a position of power in the normal way; and neglect of small matters (10), such as gradual decrease in a property qualification leading eventually to a qualitative change in the constitution. The last is dissimilarity of elements (11). This is a broad category including a number of different dissimilarities which can produce friction and disorder within a community. The main one is difference in tribe or stock. The existence of groups of dissimilar origins within a community provides a focus for political strife. Aristotle is not thinking here of racial differences, such as the difference between Greeks and barbarians, though such divisions would certainly cause difficulties within a community, but is referring to the differences that can exist between Greeks of different cities, with different tribal origins and communal traditions. When colonies or new cities are formed

[18] V.3.ix–xvi (1303 ^{a} 13–^{b} 17) 195–7.

with citizens from more than one city, this difference in background may be perpetuated in political factions and may prevent the citizens from uniting into a harmonious civic body. Another difference which may cause dissension is that of geographical terrain. In the state of Athens, for example, there is tension because the inhabitants of the port, Piraeus, are more democratic in outlook than the inhabitants of the city itself.

Aristotle distinguishes these four causes from the earlier seven by saying that 'from one point of view', there are seven causes 'but from another point of view more'[19] but he does not explain the point of this distinction. It is not simply a question of whether change is accompanied by *stasis*, because, though some of the second group of causes produce peaceful change without *stasis*, the last cause, dissimilarity of population or topography, is definitely a cause of *stasis* between different groups in the state. This cause, however, differs from the first seven causes of *stasis* in having its origins more in the actual foundation of the community than in the subsequent behaviour of the rulers or their subjects. Perhaps, therefore, by classifying this cause with the unintentional and accidental causes of change, Aristotle wishes to distinguish the more remote and indirect causes from the more immediate and direct. But this distinction is not a clear one; disproportionate increase, for example, is a relatively remote and indirect cause of dissension and yet is included in the first group. Aristotle seems to be more concerned to identify and describe the different causes of change and *stasis* than to classify them systematically into clearly differentiated groups.

Further classification of these eleven causes has been attempted by modern commentators. It has been argued, for example, that of the initial seven causes, the first four affect those who are excluded from power while the other three affect those who are in power. Profit, honour, *hybris,* and pre-eminence refer to the characteristics and behaviour of the rulers which provoke their subjects; fear, contempt, and disproportionate increase are conditions of the powerless which cause them to rebel. This distinction, however, is not as clear as it might appear because Aristotle's categories are not completely distinct. Fear on the part of the ruled, for example, may be caused by the *hybris* of the rulers; or contempt for those in power may be provoked by their apparently wrongful possession of honour. None the less, the distinction may serve to underline an important point of difference between

---

[19] V.2.iv (1302 a 34–7) 193.

Aristotle and Plato. Plato had said that constitutional change was always due to dissension within the ruling class whereas Aristotle believes that it may originate from any quarter of the community.

It may be more useful to classify the different causes into the following three groups: first, those causes which depend on the particular behaviour of the rulers and on the emotional response of their subjects; for example, *hybris*, contempt, or fear; secondly, what may be called 'social' causes, where dissidence is caused by some factor in the basic social structure of the community, for example a citizen body drawn from members of incompatible populations or the relative increase of one class from economic or other reasons; thirdly those causes which operate almost unnoticed because of the negligence of the rulers or the gradualness of the change. Again the classification is not clear cut and we must remember that it is not made by Aristotle himself. But it does at least indicate the great variety of the causes he lists. One of the main purposes of his account of *stasis* and change is to point out the variety of their origins. That his list of causes defies clear and systematic classification either by himself or by his commentators may perhaps be seen as a measure of his success in demonstrating the complexity of the subject.

Aristotle's analysis of the general causes of *stasis* and constitutional change does not, as we might expect, end at this point. He adds a further chapter[20] which includes a number of supplementary observations in a somewhat random order. Some are additional comments or glosses on points made in the previous chapter. For example, he cites more examples of how relative growth of one part of the community may lead to a change in the constitution[21] and emphasizes the ways in which members of groups who have achieved positions of power may provoke opposition and rebellion.[22] But new material is also introduced. A new and important distinction is made between the origins or occasions of *stasis* (literally, 'the things out of which *stasis* comes) and the issues at stake (literally, 'the things about which *stasis* takes place'). The former may be small but the latter are always great and Aristotle gives some interesting examples of revolutions which have begun from trivial incidents such as marriages or lovers' tiffs.[23] These incidents are both more immediate and at the same time less obviously causes of *stasis* than any of the earlier eleven causes. The distinction between occasions and issues is still a useful one; when accounting for some

[20] V.4. [21] V.4.viii–ix (1304 ^{a} 17–33) 198–9.

[22] V.4.x (1304 ^{a} 33–8) 199.

[23] V.4.i–vii (1303 ^{b} 17–1304 ^{a} 17) 197–8.

major political upheaval, we shall often want to distinguish the major, underlying causes from the more immediate occasions or 'trigger-factors'. Aristotle also distinguishes between the different means by which changes may be effected or power seized.[24] The main means are force and fraud, each of which is then further subdivided. Force may be used either from the beginning or later; fraud may be used initially and then the people held down by force or persuasion may be sufficient both for the seizure and for the subsequent maintenance of power. We have already seen cases where the constitution changes though no one has intended a change. Now we have an intermediate possibility, change which is deliberate and intentional but carried through without violence. Like the distinction between occasions and issues, the distinction between force and fraud cuts across all the previous distinctions and provides one more aspect of *stasis* and change which must be examined as part of the over-all explanation of any particular instance.

By these additions Aristotle has undoubtedly blurred the elegance and simplicity of his earlier analysis of causes into three major categories with eleven types in the third category. If he had reorganized his material and incorporated the new distinctions into the original classification, he could have made his account more systematic. That he has not done so, even in a section of the *Politics* which is comparatively well organized, illustrates his approach to political science and indeed to all areas of scientific inquiry. His major aim, in politics or biology or any other subject, is to describe and explain the given subject matter in all its complexity. The urge to distinguish and to avoid over-simplification is almost an obsession. The ultimate objective may be to incorporate all these distinctions in any one subject into one coherent body of knowledge moving systematically from the more general to the more particular. But the immediate and more pressing task is to make sure that no relevant distinction is passed over. His mind is so open to new evidence and new distinctions that he is always prepared to use them to subvert not only other people's schemes and classifications but also his own. This process of constant revision can be seen in the classification of constitutions and is even more evident in the analysis of the general causes of *stasis* and constitutional change. It may make his ideas difficult to grasp but we must respect his openmindedness and his willingness to revise his own theories in the face of new evidence.

[24] V.4.xii–xiii (1304 b 7–18) 199–200.

Causes in particular constitutions

The next stage is to list causes for individual types of constitution. Democracy and oligarchy, as the two commonest forms of constitution, are treated first and at greatest length.[25] Aristocracy and polity are then taken together.[26] By 'aristocracy' Aristotle means not the ideal rule of the virtuous but so-called aristocracy, the mixture of birth, wealth, and poverty. He can thus include aristocracy with polity because both are species of mixed constitution and are closely related. As he knows few examples of these two types, he would have had difficulty in filling out a reasonable section for each. These sections are mostly concerned with causes of *stasis* and constitutional change which are peculiar to the particular type. Thus, in the chapter on democracy, we hear much of the activity of the demagogue, the popular leader particularly associated with democracy, though Aristotle later broadens the concept of demagogy to include similar behaviour within a more restricted group than the people as a whole.[27] In the case of oligarchy he emphasizes dissension within the ruling class, a fault to which he thinks oligarchies are especially prone. In the case of aristocracies and polities, the mixed constitutions, he concentrates on factors which may change the constitution by altering the balance of the mixture, for example, grasping behaviour of the nobles. Some factors are mentioned in these chapters which might have qualified as general causes. In particular, he refers for the first time to external factors, the influence of foreign states:

Constitutions may be changed from the outside as well as from within; for example, if a neighbouring constitution is of the opposite kind and is not far away, or, if far away, especially powerful. Both the Athenians and the Spartans illustrate this in their history; the Athenians everywhere brought low the oligarchies, the Spartans the popular governments.[28]

The bulk of these chapters is taken up with historical examples which demonstrate Aristotle's wide knowledge of Greek politics and his ability to marshall this knowledge to illustrate general points. Detailed discussion of this historical evidence is beyond the scope of this study, but we should remember that our concentration on the more general aspects of Aristotle's analysis can provide only a partial and one-sided picture of his work.

Monarchy, that is kingship and tyranny, is treated separately from

[25] V.5; V.6. [26] V.7.
[27] V.6.vi–vii (1305 b 23–39) 203.
[28] V.7.xiv (1307 b 19–24) 208.

the other four constitutions but we may conveniently include the causes
of constitutional change and *stasis* in monarchies[29] under the heading
of causes in particular constitutions. In general, the same causes which
affect the other constitutions also affect kingship and tyranny,[30] for
example, *hybris,* fear and contempt. Individual ambition is also a cause,
especially the ambition to win glory by the assassination of a tyrant.
Tyranny is particularly susceptible to external attack from hostile
neighbours. Those tyrants who have not won their position for themselves but have inherited it from someone else are likely to be overthrown because they have been brought up in softness and luxury.
Because tyranny combines the evils of both extreme democracy and
extreme oligarchy it is liable to be overthrown by the same causes as
each of these types, presumably by the oppression of the rich or of the
poor, the respective vices of extreme democracy and extreme oligarchy.
In kingship, which is less open to external attack, there are two main
causes of change: conflict within the royal family and illegal action by
the king himself. Again, as with the other constitutions, the major
interest lies in the wealth of examples Aristotle has amassed even of
forms of government which he admits are relatively rare in his own time.

During the discussion of causes in particular types of constitution,
Aristotle also refers to possible patterns or cycles of change. Plato, in
the *Republic,* had described a pattern of change from timocracy on the
Spartan model through oligarchy and democracy to tyranny and the
question of what constitutions tend to change into what other constitutions is one of the general topics announced at the beginning of Book
Five.[31] Aristotle has already given two generalized accounts, broadly
similar, of Greek constitutional development from kingship to democracy.[32] But they are historical in purpose and are not meant to have
theoretical or predictive value. As we would expect, he is aware of the
great variety of actual and possible changes and is sceptical of simple
schemes like Plato's. His general principle is that the commonest type of
constitutional change is change into the opposite form, though it is not
always clear precisely what this means. 'Opposite' is sometimes to be
understood in terms of the distinction between normal or perverted
constitutions; a constitution's opposite form is a constitution with a
ruling group of the same size (one, few or many) but normal instead of
perverted or *vice versa.* This type of change into opposites appears in
the *Ethics* where Aristotle describes how kingship passes into tyranny,

    [29] V.10.   [30] Cf. V.10.i (1310 a 40–b 2) 217.
    [31] V.1.i (1301 a 22) 189.
    [32] III.15.xi–xiii (1286 b 8–22) 140–1; IV.13.x–xi (1297 b 16–28) 178.

aristocracy into oligarchy, and 'timocracy' (polity) into democracy.[33] Change of this type is easy because it requires little if any structural change in the legal or constitutional machinery of government but is simply a result of a change in the moral character of the rulers. He does not mention the possibility of a reverse change, from the perverted to the normal, which would be just as easy constitutionally. In general, he tends to share Plato's pessimism about people in power and believes that change is usually for the worse. In the *Politics* 'opposite' sometimes refers to the division between rich and poor; change to an opposite constitution is thus change from aristocracy and oligarchy to democracy or from polity and democracy to oligarchy.[34] But Aristotle is now less interested in stating general principles than in pointing out exceptions. Any simple scheme could not stand in the face of his growing recognition of the great variety of constitutions and of patterns of change. When he is explicitly arguing against Plato he is particularly hostile towards the notion of universal patterns of change. Democracy may change into oligarchy instead of into tyranny; oligarchy may change into tyranny rather than in to democracy; history shows that tyranny may change into another tyranny or into oligarchy or into democracy or into aristocracy.[35] We are left with the impression that any simple cycle or scheme, even the one he himself describes in the *Ethics,* will be so riddled with qualifications and exceptions as to be virtually worthless. This is confirmed by the fact that, though he announces the general question of patterns of change at the beginning of Book Five, he does not deal with it constructively or systematically but contents himself with passing remarks which are all destructive in intent.

Methods of Prevention

The main purpose of analysing the causes of constitutional change and *stasis* is to teach the statesman how to preserve the stability of his constitution. The discussion of causes is followed immediately by discussion of methods of prevention and almost all the advice that Aristotle gives can be traced directly back to statements in the analysis of causes. Indeed, there are occasions during the causal analysis itself when the practical consequences are referred to immediately.[36] Like the causes, the preventive measures come in differing degrees of general-

[33] *EN* VIII.10 (1160 ^{b} 7–22); cf. V.10.xxx (1312 ^{b} 6–7) 222; V.12.x (1316 ^{a} 18–20) 233.

[34] V.7.viii (1307 ^{a} 20–7) 207; cf. V.6.xviii (1306 ^{b} 17–21) 205.

[35] V.12.xi–xiii (1316 ^{a} 24–39) 233.

[36] e.g. V.4.iii (1303 ^{b} 26–8) 197.

ity. Aristotle begins with general principles affecting all constitutions
and then refers to the major types of constitution, especially oligarchy
and democracy. Next, after discussing the causes of change and *stasis* in
monarchies, he gives advice about how to preserve the types of monarchy, kingship and tyranny. Finally, in Book Six, he recommends
measures for preserving the different species of democracy and oligarchy.

That he recommends methods of preserving all types of constitution,
even those which he considers most pernicious, may seem surprising and
requires some explanation. He certainly adopts an attitude of strict
ethical neutrality and seems to have relished the intellectual challenge
of entering into the spirit of different types of constitution. On the
surface, then, he appears to be the complete 'machiavel' and to have
altogether suppressed his own moral convictions. But this picture is not
completely accurate. Political disorder threatens the life and property
of individuals and therefore prevents them from living the good life, as
Aristotle conceives it. Political stability is therefore closely linked to his
own values. But this general preference for stability may not be sufficient to justify the preservation of all regimes regardless of their
merit. There will surely be some political situations where the security
of individual citizens will be better protected, at least in the long run,
by an improvement and therefore a change in the type of government.
The worst forms of constitution, such as tyranny or extreme oligarchy
or extreme democracy, are essentially hostile to the life and property
of their subjects; we would therefore expect Aristotle to be in favour
of the destruction not the preservation of such regimes. He himself
provides two indirect answers to this objection. First, outright rebellion
and seizure of power by the men of virtue, though justifiable, is not a
practical possibility.

Those members who are of outstanding merit would have by far the
greatest justification for rebelling, but they least often do so.[37]

Thus the prevention of all revolution will not prevent revolution by the
virtuous because such men will not rebel anyway. Secondly, as we shall
see, much of the advice he gives, especially to the worst forms of government, requires the use of measures which will in fact make the regimes
better by his own standards. Though he argues that the reason for
adopting such measures is that they preserve the particular constitutions
and are therefore in the ruler's own interests, the fact that they are also

[37] V.1.vi (1301 a 39–40) 190.

measures which improve the constitution lessens the apparent inconsistency between his own values and those of the rulers he advises. The inconsistency is not removed completely but it is not as glaring as it at first sight appears.

The main principle to be followed in preserving constitutions is to ensure that 'the loyal citizens should be stronger than the disloyal'.[38] This is closely connected with the principle of moderation, because many of the methods recommended for gaining loyalty and consent amount to the pursuit of moderation and the avoidance of extremes. The surest way for rulers to make their subjects loyal is to treat them well. For example, in oligarchies the rich should not maltreat the poor and should be particularly careful not to enrich themselves by virtue of their position of power.[39] Oligarchies should also be prepared to admit deserving individuals to their ranks.[40] Conversely, democracies should treat the rich well. The rich will be content if their property is not divided among the poor and if they are not heavily taxed or made to undertake expensive public services. Similar advice is given in Book Six, in the discussion of how to preserve the different species of democracy and oligarchy. Democracies should avoid confiscating the property of the rich or victimizing them in public trials.[41] Oligarchs should willingly accept onerous public services and should placate the people with generous public expenditure on such things as festivals and public buildings.[42]

The general effect of these measures, which are aimed at gaining the support of those excluded from power, will be to temper the constitution by moderating the divisions and conflicts between the opposing groups of rich and poor. This illustrates an important distinction: the principles which support and preserve a constitution are not necessarily the same as those on which the constitution is itself based and which determine the distribution of power and the values of the ruling class. Indeed the dominant principles of the constitution may work against its continued existence.

Many steps, apparently democratic, may be taken that lead to the fall of a democracy and the same may happen in oligarchies. . . . Therefore both the lawgivers and the practising politician must learn to distinguish between those democratic measures which preserve and those which undermine democracy and oligarchic measures in the same way.[43]

[38] V.9.v (1309 ^{b} 16–18) 214; cf. IV.12.i (1296 ^{b} 15–16) 175.
[39] V.8.xvi (1308 ^{b} 33–8) 212.   [40] V.8.v (1308 ^{a} 8–9) 209.
[41] VI.5.iii–iv (1320 ^{a} 6–17) 245.   [42] VI.7.v–vi (1321 ^{a} 31–40) 249.
[43] V.9.vi; ix (1309 ^{b} 20–1; 35–7) 214; 215.

To make their subjects contented and loyal democrats must in certain respects become less democratic and oligarchs less oligarchic.

Aristotle is opposed to any dishonest engineering of the subjects' consent and refers to his earlier criticism of the clever devices or 'sophistries' by which oligarchs deceive the poor and democrats the rich.[44] For example, oligarchs may make the assembly or the courts open to all but at the same time may impose a fine on those wealthy men who do not attend, thus ensuring a proportionately higher attendance from the rich than from the poor. Conversely, democracies, by offering payment for attendance but not fining the rich for non-attendance, ensure an assembly dominated by the poor though they claim it is open to all. Aristotle claims that such deceit, which gives the appearance, but not the reality, of power, will be useless,[45] presumably because people will see through it. But he does not give any supporting evidence and we may wonder whether the claim is justified. The example he gives of a democratic device, payment for attendance without a corresponding fine for the rich, was the normal practice in democratic Athens which was a relatively stable constitution by Greek standards. Aristotle's objections may be moral rather than empirical. Because he disapproves of such measures he may be too ready to believe that they are in fact useless as means of ensuring consent and stability. Some of the measures that he himself later recommends come very close to being deceptive. For example,

Constitutions last longer not only when any possible destroyers are at a distance, but sometimes just because they are close by; for through fear of them men keep a firm hold on their own constitution. So it becomes the duty of those who have the interests of the constitution at heart to create fear on its behalf, so that all may be on the lookout and not allow their watch on the constitution to disperse like sentries at night; the distant fear must be brought home.[46]

This device of exaggerating the threat from outside in order to increase internal unity (a device still widely used by regimes which feel insecure) is surely deceitful. In his advice to the tyrant Aristotle is also forced to rely to a considerable extent on measures involving deception. On the whole, however, he keeps to the principle that a government, to be secure, should not just appear to treat its subjects well but should actually do so.

As well as protecting the material condition of their subjects, the

[44] IV.13.i–vi (1297 a 14–b 1) 176–7.
[45] V.8.iv (1308 a 1–2) 209.   [46] V.8.viii (1308 a 24–30) 210.

rulers should also pay attention to their values and attitudes. Ideas or behaviour which may lead to disrespect for the constitution and its laws are to be avoided. The system of education, which most states ignore, must be made to support and not undermine the constitution. Education is a vital factor not only in the ideal state but in any state which wishes to preserve its constitution.

It is useless to have the most beneficial rules of society fully agreed upon by all members of the constitution, if individuals are not going to be trained and have their habits formed for that constitution, that is to live democratically if the laws of society are democratic, oligarch-ically if they are oligarchic;[47]

Though education should be relative to the constitution concerned, this does not mean that it should concentrate solely on inculcating the values of the ruling class. Again the rulers must distinguish between those of their principles which preserve, and those which destroy, their constitution.[48] Aristotle does not give any details of what should be included in the proper education for each constitution but he does mention certain ideas and values which are to be avoided. Oligarchs, for example, should be wary of educating their own sons to a life of luxury. Such a life may accord with the oligarchic emphasis on the value of wealth but it will make the ruling class soft and liable to be overthrown, especially if the poor are at the same time being toughened by hard work and exercise. It is in this context that he makes his well-known criticism of the democratic conception of freedom. The democratic notion that freedom is doing what one likes may work against democ-racy and lead to the destruction of the constitution, by encouraging anarchy and disrespect for the law.

It ought not to be regarded as slavery to have to live according to the constitution but rather as self-preservation.[49]

Thus Aristotle's advice to oligarchs and democrats of the more extreme type is that they should become more moderate. Such advice fits with his general conviction that, ideal situations excepted, political extremism is inherently more unstable than government based on a mixture of principles. This conviction, which provides one of the main reasons for the relative superiority of the polity in comparison with the unmixed forms of oligarchy and democracy, may have some empirical

[47] V.9.xii (1310 a 14–18) 216; cf. V.8.xiii (1308 b 20–4) 211.
[48] V.9.xiii (1310 a 19–23) 216.
[49] V.9.xvi (1310 a 34–6) 216.

justification and Aristotle's advice may be politically sound. But it
causes a problem in relation to his stated intention of preserving all
types of constitution. If an extreme oligarchy or democracy is to
become more moderate, will this not amount to a change in the constitution rather than a means of preserving it? 'Change or perish' may
be the right political advice for such regimes but can a constitution be
said to be preserved by being changed? The problem does not arise
sharply so long as Aristotle confines his remarks to the general categories
of oligarchy and democracy. At this level of generality, a moderate
oligarchy is still an oligarchy and a moderate democracy still a democracy and Aristotle sometimes does not consider the change from one
sub-type to another to be a genuine instance of constitutional change.[50]
Usually, however, he does count such changes as changes in the constitution. In Book Six, when he makes recommendations about the construc-
tion and preservation of each of the different species of democracy and
oligarchy, the difficulty is particularly acute. Though he undertakes to
preserve extreme democracy and extreme oligarchy, the measures he
favours tend to make the constitutions more moderate and therefore
different. This inconsistency makes these sections unreal and unconvincing. Extreme democrats, for example, are advised not to deprive the
rich of their property even if this means holding few assemblies or public
trials which cost money because those who attend have to be paid.[51]
Such docility and moderation on the part of the poor majority is hardly
characteristic of extreme democracy as Aristotle describes it elsewhere.
In the case of extreme oligarchy, he does not make any specific recommendations but simply offers the vague injunction that the worst forms
of government require the greatest care and vigilance.[52]

The same problem arises, though in a slightly different form, in connection with the other type of extreme and perverted rule, tyranny.
Aristotle describes two contrasting methods of preserving tyranny, of
which the first is derived from the practice of the tyrants of early Greek
history and of the Persian kings.[53] It involves such expedients as the
assassination of rivals, depriving the citizens of their wealth and keeping
them hard at work without leisure or education, encouraging flatterers,
and despising people of noble character. It can be summed up in three
precepts: humiliate one's subjects, make them distrust one another and

[50] V.1.ix (1301 b 13–17) 190.
[51] VI.5.v–vi (1320 a 17–29) 245–6.
[52] VI.6.iii–iv (1320 b 30–1321 a 1) 247.
[53] V.11.iv–xvi (1313 a 34–1314 a 29) 225–7.

make them incapable of action. The second, opposite, method follows
from Aristotle's own inquiry into the causes of *stasis* and constitutional
change in monarchies.[54] Just as a kingship is destroyed by tending
towards tyranny, so a tyranny will be preserved by tending towards
kingship. The tyrant must behave like a king, provided that he keeps
sufficient power to dominate his subjects whether they like him or not;
if he abandons this power, he will no longer be a tyrant. He should
therefore avoid acts of *hybris* and sexual violation of his subjects and
should maintain the appearance of personal virtue and respect for public
funds. He should honour the virtuous among his subjects and should
administer justice through the courts. Of these two opposing methods,
the first is described, somewhat dismissively, as the 'traditional' method
and Aristotle does not himself vouch for its efficacy. It is the second
method, derived from his own causal analysis, which he supports. Not
only will it make tyrannies more lasting; it will also make them better.
The tyrant's rule will therefore be

better and more enviable; it will not be hated and feared and it will be
exercised over better men, not men reduced to impotent submission.[55]

Thus, as in the cases of extreme oligarchy and democracy, the regime
is to be maintained by being made more moderate. The difference is
that Aristotle is aware of an alternative method which would tend to
make the tyrant's regime not less but more extreme. Perhaps he is too
ready to dismiss this method as ineffective. Like many who oppose
police states on moral grounds, he is eager to believe that such regimes
are unlikely to last and that it is in the rulers' own interests to treat
their subjects more liberally and justly. Even if we accept that moderation is more effective than ruthless extremism for preserving the
tyrant, the problem of identity and change remains: is the moderate
tyrant still a tyrant? Aristotle himself seems to recognize the difficulty
and is careful to insist that the moderate tyrant must retain some tyrannical characteristics. He must keep enough power to control his subjects
should they not consent to his rule. Also, the virtue and generosity of
the moderate tyrant is to be apparent and not genuine. He must give
the *appearance* of being concerned for the public funds, a brave soldier,
self-controlled and respectful of religion. But even if he retains power
and lacks genuine virtue, the character of his rule will still have been
substantially altered. His behaviour, if not his motives, will be kingly

[54] V.11. xvii–xxxiv (1314 a 29–1315 b 10) 228–31.
[55] V.11.xxxiv (1315 b 5–7) 231.

rather than tyrannical. Above all, his subjects will consent to his rule
and the difference between rule with and without consent is the main
criterion for distinguishing kingship from tyranny. The task that Aristotle
has set himself is in fact impossible. Believing that extreme constitutions
are inherently unstable, he is unwilling to support means of making
them stable which do not also involve making them less extreme and so
altering their character. One wishes that he had recognized this inconsistency and had consciously abandoned the attempt to preserve every
type of constitution whatsoever. By so doing, he would not have been
abandoning his aim of showing that political science has advice to give
the statesman in every type of political situation. He certainly has
advice to give extreme oligarchs, democrats, and tyrants but he should
have admitted more openly that he considers their position untenable
and that they must change the nature of their rule or be overthrown.

The same variety and attention to detail which mark the causal
analysis are evident in the methods of preservation. Two points may be
briefly mentioned to illustrate the close correspondence between the
causes and the recommendations and also the difficulty of preventing
all constitutional change. First, as change often starts from small
beginnings, the rulers must be on their watch for apparently innocuous
incidents. This requires exceptional skill and vigilance because only 'a
real statesman can discern in its early stages harm that is being done'.[56]
Secondly, the rulers must also guard against changes which occur, often
gradually, in the general economic and social structure of the community.
Where there are property qualifications for office, the level of the
qualifications should be frequently reviewed in order to prevent any
change in the composition of the ruling class caused by alteration in the
general economic wealth of the community.[57] Relative changes in the
prosperity of individuals or classes must be watched. In the case of
individuals who become excessively prosperous, Aristotle recommends
banishment as a last resort[58] and again shows his willingness to sacrifice
the individual for the general good of the community. Where a considerable section of the community becomes relatively more wealthy, the
drastic measure of banishment is not possible. Instead, he suggests a
number of general measures, all of which have the effect of making the
constitution a mixed one:

The danger can be met by not entrusting assignments and responsibilities
to one section alone but to different and opposing sections. (I am

---

[56] V.8.ix (1308 a 33–5) 210.   [57] V.8.x–xi (1308 a 35–b 10) 210–11.
[58] V.8.xii (1308 b 19) 211; cf. V.3.iii (1302 b 17–21) 193–4.

opposing the educated class to the generality and the wealthy to the more indigent.) An endeavour should be made either to merge the poorer with the richer or to augment the number of those of medium wealth.[59]

By recommending a mixture of elements in the constitution, Aristotle implies that the way to deal with the relative growth of one section of the community will be to give this section a greater share in the constitution. In effect, if the community is to remain politically stable, the constitution will have to be changed. This fits with his belief that political stability is possible only if the distribution of power is in harmony with the general social and economic structure of the community. But, though his advice may make good political sense, he is again implicitly recognized that not all constitutions are salvageable. Because the statesman cannot exercise complete control over the relative distribution of wealth, he is not always free to preserve the relative distribution of power.

Aristotle's recommendations about the preservation of constitutions accord both with his analysis of the causes of *stasis* and constitutional change and with his convictions about the conditions necessary for political stability. Though he deals with the politics of the Greek city-states much of his advice may be readily transferred to other political contexts which indicates both the continuity of political experience and Aristotle's success in generalizing from his evidence. Two major objections have emerged. First, he is perhaps too sanguine about the inability of political regimes to perpetuate their rule by immoderate and unjust means. But this question is at least open to debate and his liberal conviction that terror and oppression are not in the ultimate interests of those who use them may have empirical as well as moral justification. The second objection is more serious because it involves an internal inconsistency in his theory. If he believes that certain constitutions are unavoidably unstable and can only be 'preserved' by being changed, he should have been prepared to qualify his aim of preserving any constitution whatsoever. The qualification required would be only slight; the number of irretrievable situations is comparatively small and even there the rulers are shown how they may still retain some, if not all, of their power.

Neither of these criticisms should be taken as objections to Aristotle's assumption that political science should be concerned with the making

[59] V.8.xiv (1308 b 25–30) 211–12.

of recommendations. Indeed, in his account of constitutional change and *stasis*, he demonstrates the validity of this assumption. If the political scientist can explain the causes of a political phenomenon which politicians wish to avoid, then he is in a position to offer expert advice. The choice of aim, we may concede, should lie with the politician rather than the political scientist. But given an agreement over ends, the political scientist can then use his expert knowledge to recommend appropriate means. Aristotle himself admits political science is an imprecise science and cannot produce explanations which lead to certain predictions. It cannot therefore provide an infallible solution for any political problem. None the less, he shows that, used sensitively and with due respect for its limitations, the discipline can yield general precepts worthy of the politician's consideration.

NOTES

Books or articles listed in the Select Bibliography are referred to by author or title only.

INTRODUCTION
p. 1. *The Composition of the* Politics. The most important theories of difference in date and philosophical development are those of Jaeger, who argues that Books Seven and Eight were written first, and von Arnim (H. von Arnim, *Zur Entstehungsgeschichte der Aristotelischen Politik* (Vienna, Leipzig, 1924)), who argues that they were written last. The assumption of an underlying unity of doctrine, if not of actual composition, is now generally accepted; see Barker (1), xli–xlvi; Sinclair (2), 237–8; R. Stark, 'Der Gesamtaufbau der Aristotelischen Politik', *La Politique d'Aristote*, 3–35.

CHAPTER ONE
p. 3. *Eudemian and Nicomachean Ethics.* The relation between the two treatises has been discussed most recently by C. J. Rowe, *The Eudemian and Nicomachean Ethics: a study in the development of Aristotle's Thought* (Cambridge, 1971), who supports the generally accepted view that the *Eudemian Ethics* is earlier than the *Nicomachean Ethics*. The two most obvious links between the *Politics* and the *Nicomachean Ethics* are the discussion of political science in the opening chapters of the *Ethics* and the summary of the contents of the *Politics* at the end of the *Ethics*. The discussion of the good life in *Politics* VII, however, may be closer to the *Eudemian Ethics*; cf. Jaeger, ch. 10 and below, note to p. 89.
p. 4 *Eudaimonia*. The Greek phrase for 'the good life', *to eu zen*, is commonly used as an equivalent for *eudaimonia*. For Aristotle's conception of the final good see Hardie, ch. 2; J. L. Ackrill, *Aristotle on Eudaimonia,* Dawes Hicks Lecture on Philosophy 1974 (London, 1975). The magnanimous man, though he will accept honours which are offered, will not be distressed if they are refused him (*EN* IV.3 (1124[a] 12–17)). For the importance of leisure and private life, as distinct from participation in politics, see Solmsen.
p. 7. *Scientific explanation.* For Aristotle's view of the nature of science in general see Randall, ch. 3; Allan, ch. 11; G. E. R. Lloyd, *Early Greek Science: Thales to Aristotle* (London, 1970), ch. 8. The different types of science are discussed at *Metaphysics* E 1; cf. *Topics* VI.6 (145[a] 15–16); *EN* VI.2–3. Aristotle distinguishes three types of scientific knowledge: theoretical, practical, and productive, though sometimes he restricts the title 'science' (*episteme*) to knowledge of eternal, necessary truths (e.g. *EN* VI.3). Practical and productive sciences are both concerned with human action but differ in that productive sciences are

directed towards the making of an object independent of the agent, for example the poet's poem or the sculptor's statue, whereas practical sciences are concerned with particular types of action which are performed for their own sake. For contingency in nature, including human nature, see Ross, 78–81.

p. 9 *Phronesis (practical wisdom).* Aristotle's main account of *phronesis* is in *EN* VI.5; 12–13; see also III.4, xvii–xviii (1277 ^{b} 25–30) 110; VII.9.v–vi (1329 ^{a} 6–17) 273–4. For a recent survey of the difficulties see Hardie, ch. 11.

CHAPTER TWO

p. 13 *Koinonia.* Aristotle does not give a complete, formal account of this concept. Newman's summary, i.41–4, is useful except that he claims, as does Barker (2), 232, that the members of a *koinonia* must be diverse. The perfect friendship, which is a species of *koinonia*, can exist only between equals and similars (*EN* VIII.3 (1156 ^{b} 7–24)). *EN* V.5 (1133 ^{a} 16–18), 'for it is not two doctors that associate for exchange, but a doctor and a farmer, or in general people who are different and equal' should be taken to refer to the commercial *koinonia* and not to the *koinonia* in general. See also Finley, 7–8.

p. 14 *Friendship.* Friendship is associated in III.9.xiii (1280 ^{b} 38–9) 121 with the 'choice to live together'. See also *EN* VIII.1; IX.12; A. W. H. Adkins, ' "Friendship" and "Self-sufficiency" in Homer and Aristotle', *Classical Quarterly*, N.S. 13 (1963), 30–45; H. Flashar, 'Ethik und Politik in der Philosophie des Aristoteles', *Gymnasium*, 78 (1971), 283–5.

p. 14 *Justice.* For the distinction between universal and particular justice see *EN* V.1. For distributive justice see *EN* V.3. Cf. Hardie ch. 10.

p. 15 *Freedom.* For Aristotle's concept of freedom see M. Pohlenz, *Freedom in Greek Life and Thought*, translated by C. Lofmark (Dordrecht, 1966), 96–102; R. G. Mulgan, 'Aristotle and the Democratic Conception of Freedom', in B. F. Harris (ed.), *Auckland Classical Essays* (Auckland/Oxford, 1970), 95–111. See below, note to p. 133.

p. 16 *The* polis *and the state.* Though the nation state is the most obvious modern parallel for Aristotle's *polis,* in some respects the modern city, though not politically autonomous, is closer to the Greek *polis* and some of Aristotle's doctrines may be relevant to urban politics; cf. N. E. Long, 'Aristotle and the Study of Local Government', *Social Research*, 24 (1957), 287–310; G. Downey, 'Aristotle as an expert on urban problems', *Talanta*, 3 (171), 56–73.

p. 18 *Aristotle's theory of nature.* For the criticism that Aristotle's view of nature illegitimately combines description and evaluation see G. Boas, 'A Basic Conflict in Aristotle's Philosophy', *American Journal of Philology,* 64 (1943), 187–93; Robinson, xvii–xxvii; T. D. Weldon, *States and Morals* (London, 1946), 72–4. For biological influences on Aristotle's ethical and political theory see G. E. R. Lloyd, 'The role of medical and biological analogies in Aristotle's ethics', *Phronesis*, 13

(1968), 68–83. Aristotle's derivation of moral and political principles from nature might suggest that he is a believer in 'natural law' or the 'law of nature'; cf. J. Ritter, *Naturrecht bei Aristoteles* (Stuttgart, 1961); W. von Leyden, 'Aristotle and the Concept of Law', *Philosophy*, 42, (1967), 1–19; L. Strauss, *Natural Right and History* (Chicago, 1953), ch. 4. But though he does briefly mention the notion of natural justice and a universal natural law (*EN* V.7; *Rhetoric* I.13 (1373 [b] 6); 15 (1375 [a] 32)) and though he clearly helped to inspire the later development of the theory of natural law by the Stoics and Aquinas, the idea of natural law as such does not play an important role in his political theory; cf. Robinson, 62.

p. 21 *Instinctive relationships*. Though Aristotle places more emphasis on the more obviously instinctive sexual impulse, he uses the term 'necessary', which in such a context excludes the possibility of choice, to refer to the relation of master and slave as well as that of man and woman; see Newman, ii.104–5. Aristotle usually contrasts natural objects with products of human choice and contrivance (e.g. *Physics* II.1) but he does not insist on this distinction in relation to human beings. His test for naturalness in human behaviour is not whether something is instinctive or impulsive but whether it uses or develops characteristics and capacities which are innate in human beings. Hence, he can argue that man needs the external coercion of law in order to fulfil his nature.

p. 22 *The ethnos*. This word usually refers to a race or people (e.g. Greeks or Persians) but Aristotle also uses it in a more political sense to mean a political community larger than the *polis*. Such 'nations' may consist either of a number of states joined in an alliance or of collections of cities or villages ruled by a king; see Newman iii.346–7. The latter type is definitely an independent political unit distinct from the *polis*. For Aristotle's interest in types of political community larger than the *polis* see R. Weil, 'Aristote et le fédéralisme', *Association G. Budé, Congrès de Lyon, Actes du Congrès* (Paris,1960), 80–8; Weil, 376–404.

p. 23 *Political animal*. See R. Brandt, 'Untersuchungen zur politischen Philosophie des Aristoteles', *Hermes*, 102 (1974), 191–6; R. G. Mulgan, 'Aristotle's Doctrine that Man is a Political Animal', *Hermes*, 102 (1974), 438–45.

p. 24 *Logos*. Aristotle also refers to man's unique characteristic of rationality in the *Ethics* (*EN* 1.7 (1097 [b] 22–1098 [a] 20)) when arguing that human happiness (*eudaimonia*) involves the use of reason in a life of virtue.

p. 25 *Lycophron and the minimal state*. Aristotle certainly attributes a liberal theory of the state to Lycophron but Lycophron need not actually have held it. Contract theories of the state in Greek political thought were concerned more with the origin of the state's authority than with the extent of state control. Aristotle may have thought that a theory such as Lycophron's implied a minimal role for the state even though the author himself did not intend it to have this implication.

See R. G. Mulgan, 'Lycophron and Greek Theories of Social Contract' forthcoming in *Journal of the History of Ideas*.

p. 29 *The parts in Plato's ideal state*. Aristotle later admits that he is unsure whether Plato intends the community of women and property for the guardians only or for everyone. If the former is true, then not only will the old evils continue in the lower class but the difference and therefore the hostility between upper and lower classes will be exacerbated (II.5.xviii–xxi (1264 ^{a} 11–32) 66). In this case, Plato is being criticized for weakening rather than increasing the unity of the state.

p. 29 *Pluralism*. For the argument that Aristotle sees politics as necessarily pluralistic see, e.g., B. Crick, *In Defence of Politics* (London, 1962), 14.

p. 30 *Parts and necessary conditions*. Aristotle sometimes describes all the different occupational functions as parts of the *polis* (IV.3.i (1289 ^{b} 27–8) 153; IV.4.ix (1290 ^{b} 38–9) 156) and certain special functions which are performed by citizens as 'more especially' parts (IV.4.xiv (1291 ^{a} 24–8) 157); strictly speaking, only the latter should have been called parts (cf. VII.8–9). See below, note to p. 94.

p. 34 *Organic theory*. The 'organic' theory plays an important part in the influential interpretations of Barker (2) and T. D. Weldon, *States and Morals* (London, 1946), 68–78. Aristotle, it should be noted, uses the Greek word *organon* in its original sense of 'tool' or 'instrument' as well as in the biological sense of 'organ'. The argument that the whole is prior to its parts is not specifically biological; though Aristotle uses the analogy of the hand and the body in I.2.xiii (1253 ^{a} 20–5) 29 he elsewhere illustrates the same point by means of the parts of the shoe (*Metaphysics* Δ 6 (1016 ^{b} 13–16) and the letters in a syllable (*Metaphysics*, Z 17 (1041 ^{b} 12–13)).

p. 36 *Political rule*. See Newman, ii.209–10; E. Braun, *Das Dritte Buch der Aristotelischen 'Politik'* (Vienna, 1965), 41–4. Aristotle sometimes describes as 'political' types of rule where there is no obvious alternation of ruling and being ruled, e.g. the rule of husband over wife (see p. 46) and aristocracy (see p. 101).

CHAPTER THREE

p. 40 *Slavery*. See Schlaifer, 192–9; O. Gigon, 'Die Sklaverei bei Aristoteles', *La Politique d'Aristote*, 247–76.

p. 40 *The self-interest of the master*. In Book One (I.2.ii (1252 ^{a} 35) 26; I.6.x (1255 ^{b} 9–12) 36–7) the slave and master are said to have the 'same interest'. This statement is ambiguous, perhaps deliberately; it may mean that master and slave are partners in a common interest or that the slave simply serves the master's interest.

p. 41 *Barbarians*. E. Badian, 'Alexander the Great and the Unity of Mankind', *Historia*, 7 (1958), 440–4, reprinted in G. T. Griffith (ed.), *Alexander the Great, the Main Problems* (Cambridge, 1966), gives a useful summary of Aristotle's attitude towards barbarians.

p. 42 *Slaves as men*. Barker (2), 366, points out the inconsistency in Aristotle's recommendation that good conduct is to be encouraged in

slaves by the promise of eventual freedom (VII.10.xiv (1330 ^{a} 32–3)
277). If slaves can become free, the difference between master and
slave can hardly be innate; cf. Newman, i.152 and note.

p. 43 *Rule of intellect over appetite.* It is difficult to understand how
this rule can be both political and kingly when these are usually different and mutually exclusive types of rule. Perhaps 'and' (*kai*) here means
'or' or Aristotle's original words have been altered; see Newman, ii.144.
At any rate, the main point, that the rule of the intellect over the
appetites is free not despotic, is clear.

p. 44 *Women.* For a more sympathetic account of Aristotle's treatment
of women see S. R. L. Clark, *Aristotle's Man* (Oxford, 1975), Appendix
B, 206–11.

p. 47 *Acquisition (*Chrematistike*).* For Aristotle's use of this term see
Newman, ii.165. In his conclusion in I.11.iv (1258 ^{b} 27–31) 47–8
Aristotle adds an intermediate class of property between natural and
unnatural, giving timber and metals as examples. Though they are
products of the earth and so natural, they are also specialized commodities, usually imported, which are not produced on the average
farm.

p. 48 *Moral effect of trade.* See Finley. For the defence of shopkeepers on the ground that their profit is payment for a social service
see Newman, i.131; Ross, 243.

p. 51 *Aristotle and economics.* Aristotle's only other passage of economic analysis is in the *Ethics* where he discusses how disparate products
are equalized by money (*EN* V.5 (1133 ^{a} 19–^{b} 28)). Finley, 5–15,
argues convincingly that Aristotle's concern in this passage is also
primarily ethical, with what values ought to be, and that he is not offering an analysis of how prices are actually determined in the market
place; cf. S. Todd Lowry, 'Aristotle's "Natural Limit" and the Economics of Price Regulation', *Greek, Roman and Byzantine Studies,* 15
(1974), 57–63. Aristotle's economic views are attacked by E. A. Havelock, *The Liberal Temper in Greek Politics* (London, 1957), 352–65;
for a critique of Havelock's approach to the *Politics* cf. Robinson, 32–3.

CHAPTER FOUR

p. 53 *Definition of citizenship.* 'Deliberative or judicial office' is a
translation of the traditional text of III.1.xii (1275 ^{b} 19) 103 followed
by most editors and translators. Robinson follows Ross's Oxford text
and adopts 'and' (*kai*) for 'or' (*e*) which makes access to both functions,
rather than just one, essential for citizenship; see E. Braun, *Das Dritte
Buch der Aristotelischen 'Politik'* (Vienna, 1965), 248. Aristotle's
remark, III.5.ix (1278 ^{a} 36) 112, that the citizen is especially the man
who 'shares in honours' has been taken to imply a more restrictive
notion of citizenship (Newman, iii.173–4; Robinson, 18; Barker (1),
107, note 1). But Aristotle is contrasting such a status with that of the
metic or resident alien which suggests that he meant 'honours' to refer
not to high office only but to all political rights. Aristotle sometimes
refers to citizens in a kingship without suggesting that they have judicial

or deliberative rights (e.g. III.14.vii (1285 ^{a} 25–7) 136); see Newman, i.229–30. He also sometimes includes membership of the fighting forces as one of the essential features of citizenship (IV.4.xiv (1291 ^{a} 24–8) 157; cf. pp. 117–19). There is, however, no need to believe that he systematically employs a double standard of citizenship, as does H. von Arnim, *Zur Entstehungsgeschichte der Aristotelischen Politik* (Vienna, 1924), 35–7. See also C. Mossé, 'La Conception du citoyen dans la Politique d'Aristote', *Eirene*, 6 (1957), 17–21.

p. 56 *Definition of constitution.* Aristotle's initial definition in III.6.i (1278 ^{b} 8–10) 113 refers to the institutional aspect only. But it is clear from the distinction between normal and perverted constitutions which is introduced in the same chapter that Aristotle regards the end which a community pursues as an equally essential part of its constitution.

p. 56 *Virtue of good man and good citizen.* For analyses of this argument and its origins see Robinson, 14–15; Barker (1), 107, note T; cf. Newman, i.569–70.

p. 57 *The deliberative and official elements.* Barker (1), lxviii, claims that 'the system of government implied in the genius of the Greek language and the terminology of Aristotle is a system in which the initiative (*arche*) of magistrates is combined with 'validation' (*kurion*) by the civic organ of deliberation'. The etymological evidence, however, is uncertain and both *arche* and *kurion* are used by Aristotle almost interchangeably to describe the general exercise of power; see R. G. Mulgan, 'Aristotle's Sovereign', *Political Studies*, 18 (1970), 518–19.

p. 60 *Classification of constitutions.* For the relation of Aristotle's classification to those of his predecessors see de Romilly.

p. 64 *Numerical and economic criteria.* Aristotle's assertion in Book Four that both number and economic class are essential criteria is criticized by Newman, iii.197; iv.158–9, and by Barker (1), 163, note 1.

p. 65 *Biological and political classification.* Aristotle himself does not seem to have held that there was any sharp difference between classification in biology and classification in political science. In one passage he explicitly compares the two as if they were fundamentally similar (IV.4.viii–xix (1290 ^{b} 25–1291 ^{b} 13) 156–8); both depend on enumerating all the possible permutations and combinations of necessary parts. This argument is primarily polemical in intent, being meant to disprove the view that there are only two types of constitution; it has no positive influence on Aristotle's own classification and is not an accurate description of his method in biology; see Newman, i.565–9; G. E. R. Lloyd, 'The Development of Aristotle's Theory of the Classification of Animals', *Phronesis*, 6 (1961), 59–81.

p. 67 *Types of constitution.* Newman's account of Aristotle's species of constitution, iv.vii–lxx, is unsurpassed.

p. 67 *Monarchy.* Aristotle usually uses 'monarchy' as a general term for rule by one man, whether kingship or tyranny. One one occasion he seems to distinguish kingship from monarchy (V.10.xxxvii (1313 ^{a} 3–5) 223–4), a passage which has not been satisfactorily explained; cf. Weil,

43. Aristotle admits that certain people have accepted tyranny (e.g. VI.4.iii (1318 ^{b} 17–20) 241) but generally, as in the second and third types of kingship, counts such consent as a kingly characteristic. p. 69 *Absolute rule and the head of the household.* The analogy is not apt in all respects and should not be pressed too closely. The rule of the head of the household includes despotic rule over slaves but Aristotle surely does not mean to suggest that the rule of the absolute king is in any way despotic; see Newman, iii.278.

p. 69 *Ideal aristocracy,* The term 'merit' (*axia*) refers sometimes to 'true' merit and sometimes to any criterion of supposed desert such as wealth or freedom; see Newman, iii.177. For a survey of the main problems in Aristotle's account of ideal aristocracy see E. Braun, 'Aristokratie und aristokratische Verfassungsform in der Aristotelischen Politik', P. Steinmetz (ed.), *Politeia und Respublica* (Wiesbaden, 1969), 148–80. Though aristocracy is not treated as fully as kingship in Book Three, there are several passages which refer directly to it: III.5.v (1278 ^{a} 15–21) 111–12; III.7.iii (1279 ^{a} 34–7) 116; III.15.x (1286 ^{b} 3–7) 140; III.17.iv (1288 ^{a} 9–12) 146. The discussion of the virtue of the good man and the good citizen in III.4, especially xiii–xviii (1277 ^{b} 7–30) 109–10, is also indirectly connected with aristocracy.

p. 71 *Sparta.* Sparta is said here (IV.7.iv (1293 ^{b} 16–18) 165) to be a mixture of aristocracy and democracy whereas elsewhere Aristotle seems to suggest that it may also have an oligarchic element; cf. II.6.xvii (1265 ^{b} 33–1266 ^{a} 1) 71–2. In IV.9.vi–ix (1294 ^{b} 14–34) 168–9, Aristotle says that Sparta is described as both oligarchy and democracy and therefore provides an example of the sort of mixture necessary for a polity, but in V.7 Sparta is clearly classified as a so-called aristocracy; cf. de Romilly, 97. For Aristotle's attitude to Sparta see E. Braun, *Die Kritik der lakedaimonischen Verfassung in den Politika des Aristoteles* (Klagenfurt, 1956); Weil, 231–44; R. A. de Laix, 'Aristotle's conception of the Spartan constitution', *Journal of the History of Philosophy*, 12 (1974), 21–30.

p. 72 *Moderate oligarchy.* The first type of oligarchy is described at IV.6.vii (1293 ^{a} 12–14) 163 as one in which 'more people have some property but not very much'. The term 'more people' is sometimes understood as 'a majority'; but it need not have this meaning which would imply that a constitution could allow citizen rights to a majority and still be an oligarchy.

p. 75 *The first, 'ideal', democracy.* Though this type is dropped from the latter typologies, it is briefly referred to at VI.2.ix (1318 ^{a} 3–10) 238 where it is called 'that which seems especially to be a democracy', a type of description elsewhere reserved for the extreme type of democracy; see also M. Chambers, 'Aristotle's "Forms of democracy",' *Transactions of the American Philological Association*, 92 (1961), 20–1. Robinson's view, 82, that equality is not an important part of Aristotle's conception of democracy is hardly consistent with VI.2.i–iv (1317 ^{b} 2–17) 236–7.

p. 76 *Polity.* Though Aristotle prefers 'timocracy' in the *Nicomachean*

Ethics he uses 'polity' in the *Eudemian Ethics*, VII.9 (1241 ^{b} 30). For the difference between a mixed and a moderate constitution see Robinson, 99–103; G. J. D. Aalders, 'Die Mischverfassung und ihre historische Dokumentation in den *Politica* des Aristoteles', *La Politique d'Aristote*, 202. The same ambiguity appears in the account of the different ways in which oligarchic and democratic elements may be combined in a polity (IV.9.ii–v (1294 ^{a} 35–^{b} 13) 168): the first and third are genuine mixtures whereas the second is more of a compromise; cf. E. Braun, 'Die Theorie der Mischverfassung bei Aristoteles', *Wiener Studien*, N.F. 1 (1967), 80–5. For the difference between polity and so-called aristocracy see W. Siegfried, *Untersuchungen zur Staatslehre des Aristoteles* (Zurich, 1942), 66–9. At III.17.iv (1288 ^{a} 14–15) 146 Aristotle says that in a polity office is distributed to the wealthy according to merit; this passage is not easily reconciled with the picture of the polity given elsewhere and may not have been written by Aristotle in this form; see Newman, i.573 and note; Barker (1), 151, note GG.

CHAPTER FIVE

p. 79 *Moral control*. For the relative autonomy of the intellectual virtues cf. C. J. Rowe, *The Eudemian and Nicomachean Ethics: a study in the development of Aristotle's Thought* (Cambridge, 1971), 34, note 8. D. J. Allan, 'Individual and State in the *Ethics* and *Politics*', *La Politique d'Aristote*, 55–85, argues that Aristotle is more liberal than the passages in *EN* V suggest. His main argument is that the doctrine of the mean implies that moral action is a matter of individual judgement. But though virtuous conduct cannot be formulated in general rules subject to no exceptions this does not imply for Aristotle any restriction of the statesman's control over the individual; see V. Johnson, 'Aristotle on Nomos', *Classical Journal*, 33 (1937–8), 351–6; R. G. Mulgan, 'Aristotle and the Democratic Conception of Freedom', in B. F. Harris (ed.), *Auckland Classical Essays* (Auckland/Oxford, 1970), 99–104; M. Ostwald, 'Was there a conception ἄγραφος νόμος in Classical Greece?', *Phronesis*, Supplement 1 (1973), 70–104. For the importance of a small population for the public control of morality cf. VII.4.vii–ix (1326 ^{a} 25–35) 265.

p. 83 *The rule of law*. F. D. Wormuth, 'Aristotle on Law', *Essays in Political Theory presented to George H. Sabine* (New York/London, 1948). 45–61, rightly emphasizes the passage in the *Rhetoric*. However, by associating the 'rule of law' with a number of doctrines which he demonstrates Aristotle did not hold, he underestimates the extent of Aristotle's commitment to the legal control of government. For Plato's arguments about the rule of law see *Statesman*, 294–300.

p. 86 *The qualities of the absolute ruler*. Political capacity is not mentioned in III.17.v (1288 ^{a} 15–19) 146 but this omission is probably due to the generally abbreviated and summary nature of the chapter. In VII.14.ii (1332 ^{b} 16–23) 285 the superiority is said to be both physical and intellectual. For the degree of difference between the absolute ruler and his subjects see R. G. Mulgan, 'A Note on Aristotle's

Absolute Ruler', *Phronesis*, 19 (1974), 66–9. When Aristotle mentions stories of the existence of sufficiently outstanding rulers in India (VII.14.iii (1332 ^{b} 23–7) 285), it is not clear whether he is referring to divine rulers or brutish subjects. We are reminded of Aristotle's supposed advice to Alexander the Great to rule the Greeks as a leader and the barbarians as a master (Plutarch, *On the Fortune of Alexander*, 6). For the argument that Alexander is not Aristotle's absolute ruler see Ehrenberg.

p. 89 *Individual and collective good*. For the identity of the good of the individual and the state in the *Ethics* see *EN* I.1–2; Hardie, 18–19. Aristotle's attempt in VII.3 to prove the superiority of the philosophical life and to reconcile it with the claims of social and political life is less satisfactory than the compromise worked out at the end of the *Ethics*. This discrepancy is probably due to the fact that the passages have different aims but it may provide evidence that this part of Book Seven was written before the *Ethics*; cf. Jaeger, 275–82. Though Aristotle argues here that peace and isolation are better for both men and individuals, he elsewhere admits that the conquest of people naturally inferior is natural and just: I.8.xii (1256 ^{b} 25–6) 40; VII.14.xxi (1333 ^{b} 38–1334 ^{a} 2) 289.

p. 91 *'Achieving one constitution'*. This statement is made much of by R. Weil, 'Aristote et le Fédéralisme', *Association G. Budé, Congrès de Lyon, Actes du Congrès*, (Paris, 1960), 80–8; cf. Weil, 404–415; Ehrenberg, 65–71; S. M. Stern, *Aristotle on the World-State* (Oxford, 1968), 48–53.

p. 94 *The elements of the polis*. The list of elements in Book Seven may be compared with the slightly different list in Book Four (IV.4); see Newman, i.97–8. In IV.3.i–iv (1289 ^{b} 27–1290 ^{a} 3) 153 Aristotle gives yet another account of the parts of the state in terms of different social institutions and classes. The relation of this account to the one that follows in the next chapter is unclear; see Newman, i.565–9.

p. 94 *Citizenship and participation*. See Newman, i.569–70; iii.429; see also above, note to p. 53.

p. 97 *Inequality of wealth*. That some of the citizens of the ideal state will not be well off can be inferred from the requirement that *syssitia* should be publicly funded to prevent the poorer citizens from being excluded (VII.10.x (1330 ^{a} 5–8) 276). Aristotle would also probably not object to the existence of some comparatively rich citizens: in the *Ethics* (IV.2) he describes the virtue of magnificence which requires great wealth.

p. 100 *Aristocracy*. For the debate about whether the ideal state of Books Seven and Eight may be called an aristocracy see the exchange between H. Sidgwick and Newman in *Classical Review*, 6 (1892), 141–4; 289–93. Cf. E. Braun, 'Aristokratie und aristokratische Verfassungsform in der Aristotelischen Politik', P. Steinmetz (ed.), *Politeia und Respublica* (Wiesbaden, 1969), 148–54; see also above, p. 69 and note.

CHAPTER SIX

p. 102 *Contents of Books Four to Six.* Aristotle gives two lists of intended questions in IV.1 and IV.2 but they are inconsistent and neither gives a wholly accurate account of the contents of these books.

p. 102 *Mixed constitution.* For a summary of Aristotle's theory and of previous Greek theories of constitutional mixture see G. J. D. Aalders, 'Die Mischverfassung und ihre historische Dokumentation in den *Politica* des Aristoteles', *La Politique d'Aristote*, 201–37.

p. 103 *Collective wisdom.* For the view that Aristotle is supporting government by discussion see Barker (1), 126, note 1. Aristotle, or his pupil if the work is not by Aristotle himself, endorses the argument in the *Constitution of Athens*, 41.2. The principle of aggregating the qualities of individual members of groups is applied several times by Aristotle in Book Three: e.g. (apart from III.11) III.15.vii–x (1286 ^{a} 26–^{b} 7) 139–40; III.16.x–xii (1287 ^{b} 11–31) 144–5; see E. Braun, 'Die Summierungstheorie des Aristoteles', *Jahreshefte des Oesterreichischen Archäologischen Institutes*, 44 (1959), 157–84.

p. 106 *The virtues of the middle class.* For criticism of Aristotle's use of the doctrine of the mean to justify the polity see Robinson, 103. For the parallel between the polity and the ideal state see W. T. Bluhm, 'The Place of the Polity in Aristotle's Theory of the Ideal State', *Journal of Politics*, 24 (1962), 743–53; Bluhm's claim, 748–9, that the middle class is as virtuous as the citizens of the ideal state is unconvincing.

p. 111 *Support for the constitution.* Those who support the constitution must simply be stronger, not as is sometimes said, e.g. by Barker (2) 489 and Sinclair (1) in his translation of the passage quoted, more, than those who oppose it; see E. Braun, 'Eine Maxime der Staatskunst in den Politika des Aristoteles', *Jahreshefte des Oesterreichischen Archäologischen Institutes*, 44 (1949), 385–98.

p. 113 *Ranking of constitutions.* See Plato, *Statesman* 300–3.

CHAPTER SEVEN

p. 116 *Constitutional change.* For a general survey of Aristotle's account of political instability see H. Ryffel, ΜΕΤΑΒΟΛΗ ΠΟΛΙΤΕΙΩΝ (Bern, 1949), 136–79. For the incompleteness of Aristotle's treatment see Newman, iv.277–8, who lists causes which are mentioned elsewhere in the *Politics* but not in Book Five.

p. 116 *Empirical evidence.* Of the accounts of the 158 constitutions attributed to Aristotle and his pupils, only one, the *Constitution of Athens*, survives. It is undoubtedly influenced by Aristotle's general theory of democracy though this theory is itself influenced by Athenian constitutional history; see J. Day and M. Chambers, *Aristotle's History of Athenian Democracy* (Berkeley and Los Angeles, 1962), criticized by N. G. L. Hammond, *Classical Review*, N.S. 14 (1964), 34–7; G. L. Cawkwell, *Journal of Hellenic Studies*, 86 (1966), 247. Aristotle's 'empiricism' in Books Four to Six was stressed by Jaeger in his attempt to identify different stages of philosophical development. For the prior influence of theory see R. Stark, 'Der Gesamtaufbau der Aristotelischen Politik',

La Politique d'Aristote, 3–35; I. Düring, *Aristoteles* (Heidelberg, 1966), 500–1. For Aristotle's unsystematic use of evidence see G. J. D. Aalders, 'Die Mischverfassung und ihre historische Dokumentation in den *Politica* des Aristoteles', *La Politique d'Aristote,* 219–37; cf. G. Huxley, 'On Aristotle's Historical Methods', *Greek, Roman and Byzantine Studies,* 13 (1972), 157–69.

p. 118 *Stasis.* For the translation 'troubles' see Wheeler, 159. Barker (1), 204, note 1, quotes Newman as saying that *stasis* is a combination 'for the attainment of some political end by legal and illegal means'. Newman's next sentence, however, imples that *stasis* is essentially illegal: 'A party is assumed to pursue its end by legal means only, whereas a *stasis* is prepared to carry its point by illegal means if necessary' (iv.284). One of the types of *stasis* without constitutional change mentioned in V.1.viii–xi (1301 ^{b} 10–26) 190–1 is the change from one species of a general type of constitution to another species of the same type, e.g. from a moderate to an extreme democracy. From what he says elsewhere in the *Politics,* especially in Book Four where he insists on the number of different constitutions, we expect Aristotle to hold that a change from a moderate to an extreme democracy involves a change of constitution. The discrepancy, however, is not serious. Though Aristotle does not at this point consider such changes to be constitutional changes he does not exclude them from consideration. Being examples of *stasis* they are still part of the subject matter being studied.

p. 122 *Political and economic causes.* Wheeler, 156, argues on the basis of V.3.xvi (1303 ^{b} 15–17) 197 ('the greatest opposition is of virtue and vice; next comes that of wealth and poverty') that Aristotle is making political causes more important than economic causes. But Aristotle's point seems simply to be that virtue and vice are more removed from one another because they are wholly different in character, whereas the rich and the poor have some similar characteristics, e.g. selfishness; see Newman, iv.318. Cf. F. Kort, 'The Quantification of Aristotle's Theory of Revolution', *American Political Science Review,* 46 (1952), 486–93.

p. 122 *The third group of causes.* These causes are described as 'causes' and 'beginnings' of *stasis* and constitutional change (V.2.iv (1302 ^{a} 34–5) 193). These are broad and general terms which Aristotle also uses to describe all three groups taken together (V.2.i (1302 ^{a} 18) 192). It is therefore misleading to translate 'causes' when used of the third group by 'occasions', as Barker does, as if Aristotle were making a clear distinction between underlying and immediate causes. This distinction is not introduced till later (V.4). Classification of the third group of causes into direct and indirect is made by Newman, iv.296, and Barker (1), 207, note. For the distinction between causes affecting rulers and causes affecting ruled see Newman, iv.296; for classification of the eleven causes into three groups see Newman, iv.275, and Wheeler, 150. See also H. Ryfell, ΜΕΤΑΒΟΛΗ ΠΟΛΙΤΕΙΩΝ (Bern, 1949) 147–51. For Plato's emphasis on the rulers see *Republic* 465b, 545d.

p. 128 *Patterns of Constitutional Change.* On Aristotle's generalized summaries of Greek history see Weil, 339—51. By taking Plato's account of constitutional change in *Republic* VIII—IX as a theory of how constitutions always change Aristotle is almost certainly misinterpreting Plato who is most unlikely to have thought that change always followed this pattern. As often, we cannot tell whether Aristotle genuinely misunderstands Plato or whether he simply finds it convenient to take Plato's account in this way. For the meaning of 'opposite' constitution in Aristotle see Newman, iv.372; 483—4.

p. 129 *Prevention of disorder.* The precise connection between individual pieces of advice and previous statements of causes is conveniently summarized by Newman, iv.569—70. Aristotle's advice that hostility with nearby states is to be encouraged involves a modification of his earlier view that constitutions are especially in danger if neighbouring states are hostile (V.7.xiv (1307 ^{b} 19—21) 208).

p. 133 *Democratic freedom.* Newman's inference, iv.411, followed by Barker (2), 355, that Aristotle would probably have defined freedom as 'obedience to rightly constituted law' is unjustified. Obedience to law is not slavery but it is not freedom either; see R. G. Mulgan, 'Aristotle and the Democratic Conception of Freedom', in B. F. Harris (ed.), *Auckland Classical Essays* (Auckland/Oxford, 1970) 106—7. Freedom, for Aristotle, is essentially a question of independent value, of being treated as an end and not as a means; the extent of submission to, or exemption from, legal control is irrelevant.

p. 135 *Preservation of tyranny.* For the influence of Aristotle's ethical views on his advice to the tyrant see H. Ryffel, ΜΕΤΑΒΟΛΗ ΠΟΛΙΤΕΙΩΝ (Bern, 1949), 168—9. The contradiction between moderation and preservation does not arise so sharply in the case of tyranny as in the case of democracy and oligarchy because Aristotle keeps the discussion of tyranny at a general level and does not undertake to preserve extreme tyranny as such but only tyranny in general. For the question whether change of sub-type counts as constitutional change see above, note to p. 118.

p. 136 *Increasing the middle class.* It is not clear how this is to be done. Newman, iv.394, refers to the regulation of inheritances (V.8.xx (1309 ^{a} 23—6) 213) but admits that this would hardly suffice; from the general context it appears that Aristotle does not believe that the statesman has complete control over the distribution of wealth.

SELECT BIBLIOGRAPHY

Works mentioned are of a more general nature and mostly in English. References to further, more specialized, reading will be found in the notes.

Translations and Commentaries

The commentary of W. L. Newman, *The Politics of Aristotle,* four volumes (Oxford, 1887–1902), does not contain a translation but its introduction, notes, appendices, and indexes provide a wealth of relevant information and acute critical judgements and it is still indispensable for detailed study of the *Politics.* The main English translations of the *Politics* are: B. Jowett (Oxford, 1885); H. Rackham (London/ Cambridge, 1932), with parallel Greek text; E. Barker (1) (Oxford, 1946), with useful introduction and notes; T. A. Sinclair (1) (London, 1962). R. Robinson provides a comparatively literal translation of Books Three and Four (Oxford, 1962), with brief but incisive introduction and commentary.

General Surveys

Useful accounts of Aristotle's political theory appear in works which cover wider topics in the history of political thought: e.g. E. Barker (2), *The Political Thought of Plato and Aristotle* (London, 1906); C. I. McIlwain, *The Growth of Political Thought in the West* (London, 1932); T. A. Sinclair (2), *A History of Greek Political Thought* (London, 1951); and also in general surveys of Aristotle's philosophy: e.g. W. D. Ross, *Aristotle,* 5th edition (London, 1949); J. H. Randall, *Aristotle* (New York, 1960); G. E. R. Lloyd, *Aristotle: the Growth and Structure of his Thought* (Cambridge, 1968); D. J. Allan, *The Philosophy of Aristotle* (London/Oxford/New York, 1970). The chapter on the *Politics* in W. Jaeger, *Aristotle,* translated by R. Robinson, 2nd edition (Oxford, 1948), is mainly concerned with the attempt to place different sections of the *Politics* at different stages in Aristotle's philosophical development. R. Weil, *Aristote et l'histoire* (Paris, 1960) concentrates on Aristotle's use of historical evidence. *La Politique d'Aristote,* Entretiens sur l'antiquité classique XI (Geneva, 1965) contains a number of articles in English, German, and French on different aspects of the *Politics.* The most recent thorough study of Aristotle's ethics is W. F. R. Hardie, *Aristotle's Ethical Theory* (Oxford, 1968).

Articles on Particular Topics

V. Ehrenberg, 'Aristotle and Alexander's empire', V. Ehrenberg, *Alexander and the Greeks* (Oxford, 1938), 62–102.
M. I. Finley, 'Aristotle and Economic Analysis', *Past and Present,* 47 (1970), 3–25.

J. de Romilly, 'Le Classement des constitutions d'Hérodote à Aristote', *Revue des Etudes Grecques,* 72 (1959), 81–99.

R. Schlaifer, 'Greek Theories of Slavery from Homer to Aristotle', *Harvard Studies in Classical Philology,* 47 (1936), 165–204, reprinted in M. I. Finley (ed.), *Slavery in Classical Antiquity* (Cambridge, 1960).

F. Solmsen, 'Leisure and Play in Aristotle's Ideal State', *Rheinisches Museum,* 107 (1964), 193–220.

M. Wheeler, 'Aristotle's analysis of the nature of the political struggle', *American Journal of Philology,* 72 (1951), 145–61.

INDEX